FURTHER DISCLOSURE

BY

VINCE SMITH

First published 2024 Copyright © Vince Smith 2024. Vince Smith has asserted his right in accordance with the Copyright, Designs & Patents Act 1988. No part of this book may be reproduced, stored in a retrieval system, or transmitted in any form or otherwise, without the author's written permission.

Cover Design by Tommy Smith @tommysmith__art Thank you, dude.

<u>*Disclaimer.*</u>
Any resemblance to persons, living or dead, should be apparent to them and those who know them.

FURTHER DISCLOSURE

VINCE SMITH

<u>Dedication</u>
For Sarah, Kathleen, Frances, Anthony, Peter and Tommy.

<u>Epigraphs</u>

"For when the one great scorer comes to mark against your name, he writes not that you won or lost but how you played the game." Grantland Rice.

"People who say it cannot be done should not interrupt those who are doing it." George Bernard Shaw

Comments

Paedophiles, armed robbers, thieves, perverts, kidnappers, blackmailers, pimps and a serial killer. These are just some of the police officers that I worked alongside during the last five decades. Vince Smith

During my career in the West Midlands police, I worked with some incredibly talented police officers who achieved much more than I could ever have done. To avoid embarrassment, I have not named either of them. Vince Smith

If your favourite book about the Police is - 'The Police Constable who lived in a house near a field with dozens of fluffy baby lambs', then this book is probably not for you. Vince Smith

I am not sure that Charles Dickens intended it to be a question, but if he did, my answer is: "It was the best of times."

"Jesus, Mary, Joseph and the wee donkey, not another bloody book." That Irish bloke from the TV programme about bent coppers.

"If you bought my Dad's first book, he'll probably try to get you to buy this one as well." -Tommy Smith.

FURTHER DISCLOSURE

CHAPTER 1

PROLOGUE

Since publishing 'Full Disclosure', I have received several messages encouraging me to continue writing and reminding me of tales I had forgotten.

Firstly, I must correct all the factual errors in 'Full Disclosure'. Hughie McGowan's ferret, who died in suspicious circumstances, was called Bertie, not Freddie. That clears that up. Many readers described my first book as a whistle-stop journey, so this is a more relaxed stroll through my time with the West Midlands Police (1979-2007). This book took me four years to write - some sixty-two years quicker than my first effort.

These exploits are additional to those in my first book. I have introduced more characters and included details about my family and national news items. Unlike my first effort, it does not contain any poetry. I wasn't sure whether to call this volume 'Final Disclosure' or "Further Disclosure". Then I remembered...

In 1993, after twelve years in the job, I was in uniform and still working shifts. To kick-start my hardly stellar career, I applied for an attachment to the Divisional Crime Support Unit - a team that investigated serious and complex crimes committed in South Birmingham. Much to my and many other people's surprise, I was successful.

After starting with my new team, the Safeways Supermarket in Acocks Green received an anonymous letter. The writer threatened to poison their milk and sugar products unless £5,000 in cash was forthcoming. The store had never received a similar threat.

Our twenty officers smoothly rolled into action. The first briefing was held at Edward Road police station in a room full of experienced detectives and a few token police constables like me. The established detectives sat in cliques and shared ashtrays. In unison, they nodded, shook their heads and took harsh drags on their cigarettes to show their support for the boss. In the absence of any available chairs, I stood and awkwardly wrote my notes on a floppy A4 writing pad. Every substantive detective had a blue hardback A4 notebook. It visually separated detectives from their 'Woodentop' colleagues. The Superintendent instructed detectives with informants to contact their 'snouts' and find out what they knew.

A hard-nosed detective who punctuated his banter with 'When I was on the Serious Crime Squad' stood with his arms folded. His only contribution to the briefing was to mutter a line heard in most episodes of *The Sweeney:* "These bastards need locking up."

Trying to think outside the box, I suggested that previous employees might be worth checking out as possible suspects. My comment triggered micro-glances and tuts from the detectives, as well as a not-that-subtle "for fuck's sake" from the Serious Crime Squad's finest. The Superintendent paused and whispered to the Detective Inspector, who looked at me, smiled and made a note in his blue notebook.

Later that week, a stack of Safeway job applications landed on my desk with a post-it note that read, '*PC Smith, for your attention: Two hundred and fifty job applications for ex-employees of Safeways, dating back five years. Best of fucking luck, Sherlock.*'

I decided to keep my mouth shut at future briefings and only speak when answering questions. I spent the next day wading through forms and making pointless notes, pretending this was not the futile exercise that some might think. Raising the occasional eyebrow and nodding fooled no one. The truth was that the applications contained nothing of importance.

Continuing with my charade, I picked up a form submitted by a young man who had only worked at Safeways for a month. He was born in Sri Lanka and listed his academic qualifications. He seemed particularly proud of his Grade C O-Level English as a Second Language (he had underlined it). The next section of the form asked, Further disclosure, if relevant? Underneath the applicant had written:

"Sadly, my Further died of cancer last year."
So 'Further Disclosure' it is. The Safeway's job remains undetected.

CHAPTER 2

TIME FOR A CHANGE

In 1979, I was twenty-two years old, married and parentally responsible for Anthony, my fourteen-year-old brother. To look after Anthony, I purchased my discharge from the British Army. After six years, the Army assessed my character as exemplary.

In fairness, Dennis Nilsen received the same evaluation from the Army when he left. Nilsen went on to murder sixteen vulnerable people between 1978 and 1983. He was a cook in the Army, and with my first-hand knowledge of the state of the grub, I propose that Dennis Nilsen's true body count may never be known.

I lived with my wife and Anthony in a council house on the Churchill estate in Redditch. I worked in the Rates Department of the Redditch District Council. The wages were rubbish, and career prospects non-existent. Each day at work was so bad I felt like I was starring in a really low-budget version of *Groundhog Day*. I needed to make some fairly drastic lifestyle changes, starting with a more interesting job and a pay rise.

One lunchtime, my brother cooked up a delicacy which, out of necessity, he had created while I was away serving Queen and Country: 'a loaf of toast.' I watched as he placed eight slices of Mother's Pride under the gas grill of the oven. Anthony explained that he had to use the gas grill as their electricity was regularly switched off because Dad never paid the bill. Anthony turned the bread and removed it when it was golden brown. He buttered each slice. He put more bread under the grill and repeated the process until we were full.

More Bear Grylls than Jamie Oliver, yet I challenge you to eat a loaf of toast and tell me you are still hungry.

Britain's first female Prime Minister, Margaret Thatcher, won the 1979 General Election by a landslide and replaced James Callaghan. The Labour Party could not compete with the force of nature that was Mrs Thatcher. So with a new broom, her detractors would say broomstick, she swept aside her political opponents. Maggie knew she had a number of battles ahead and would require the backing of the Police. A pay rise ensured she had their full support.

I had no idea what a career in the police entailed, but it had to be an improvement. Police forces needed to replace the officers who had left because of the previously poor pay and conditions. I sent off my application and waited.

A response arrived three weeks later. It was a thick envelope, which was always a good sign (wafer-thin job application replies were almost always a rejection.) The letter notified me of my interview date.

I wore a suit, shirt, tie, and well-polished shoes for the interview. I sported a full beard and metal-framed spectacles, hoping to convince the panel that I was mature and educated.

Two weeks after my interview, the West Midlands police confirmed my start date. I immediately gave

Redditch Council notice of my intention to leave. In retrospect, perhaps I should have stayed: time there passed so slowly that I would probably only be about twenty-four years old by now.

Mum left home to escape being my Dad's Friday night boxing sparring partner. I will never understand why she never took Anthony with her. Mum lived in Hereford with her new partner and my lovely little sister Frances, who was four years my junior. My father lived in a flat in Redditch town centre. When I needed to speak to him, I called the Sportsman's Arms payphone, asking whoever answered to put my Dad on the phone. He was always there.

My sister Kathleen, two years younger than me, grew up far too quickly. Initially, she flitted between our parents' houses, but eventually, she joined her friends in hippy communes and squats. Kathleen was a beautiful free spirit and a talented artist. While in her teens, Kathleen had a son, Matthew. He was taken into care by social services; I never met him as I was in the Army serving in Germany.

My father rarely worked and said he was concerned that Frances's child maintenance could increase. He never paid a penny, so his excuse was pretty flimsy. Before I left the Army, Mum sent Anthony cards on his birthday and Christmas. She stapled a £10 note to the cards, but only the staple remained when our Dad handed my brother the card. A school friend explained what the staple meant; Anthony was disappointed but hardly surprised. My parents' separation had been bitter and attritional and continued until long after 'death did they part.'

In September 1979, with sixty-five other wide-eyed and smartly dressed recruits, I attended an induction fortnight at Bournville Lane. I filled in forms and signed up for insurance, savings, and the police federation. Ex-cadets and those with family in the police had some idea about the job. The rest of us had a lot to learn. Instructors lectured us about our behaviour and explained how the Police Regulations dangled over us like the Sword of Damocles.

It wasn't their fault, but I disliked the recruits from Coventry. At 3pm every day, they caught a bus that delivered them to Little Park Street, Coventry, while the rest of us remained in class until 4.30pm. During the day, I let the Coventry contingent know they had missed some important stuff by leaving early. The truth was they hadn't.

On Thursday of our first week, my intake attended the clothing stores to collect our uniforms. Unfortunately, they only had two sizes: Too big ("Don't worry, you will grow into it") or too small ("You could do with losing a bit of weight, to be honest, officer.")

Guest speakers rolled out anecdotal yarns of their heroics. One guy, a *Charles Hawtrey* doppelgänger, regaled our class with his tale. As a policeman, he had single-handedly arrested sixty rioting passengers on a double-decker bus in the centre of Birmingham. Some of our intake were impressed. Rod Lee, a big lad with a brother in the job, shook his head and muttered,

"What a load of bollocks - I don't think he could climb the stairs on a bus without a rope and a grappling hook."

Personal likes, dislikes and friendships developed over lunch and smoke breaks. The instructors paused classes every thirty minutes to allow gasping smokers a much-needed fag. There were many reasons why I never smoked, but perhaps the most compelling was a childhood aversion.

While attending Our Lady's Junior School in Hereford, the janitor would leave a crate containing twenty-four 1/3-pint bottles of pasteurised milk outside each classroom every morning. When the bell for the first break sounded, the milk monitor sprang into action, handing out bottles of milk and straws. My form teacher, Mr Michael, joined the milk drinkers. He would roll a cigarette, light up and fill the classroom with the overpowering smell of *Old Holborn* tobacco. When blended with the taste of milk, the smell almost made me throw up. As a result, I neither smoked nor drank milk.

During the second week of our course, my class swore allegiance to Her Majesty the Queen, and we became probationary constables. A police officer's probation lasted two years. During that period, it was not difficult for the organisation to dispense with the services of the unwanted.

On the third week, we relocated to the Regional Police Training College at Ryton-on-Dunsmore for a further ten weeks of training. Unfortunately for those from Coventry, the course was residential, so they no longer had a 3pm finish.

At Ryton, my intake had eight classes of twenty-four students aged between eighteen and forty. My course had twice the number of males as females. The class timetable contained the activities pictured on the recruiting brochure: drill, first-aid, self-defence and life-saving.

At the start of the course, each student had to stand at the front of the class and give a talk about themselves. Rod Lee hunched up a bit during his speech. Sergeant Bob Duxbury, our instructor, asked Rod who was the tallest in our class if he was conscious about his size. Rod laughed and explained he was more concerned about how small he was, explaining that his brothers all towered over him.

Swimming life-saving lessons took place in a small, not-deep-enough-to-have-to-swim pool. My upper body performed the front crawl while my legs bounced like a kangaroo on crystal meth. I bobbed my way through my life-saving qualifications.

As students, we maintained a practice pocketbook for ten weeks. Before my course, trainers told officers to write their notes at the time. Tragically, that instruction cost a young policeman his life.

On a night shift in Leicester, a lone officer witnessed a burglary at a factory unit. He didn't contact the controller and started writing the details in his pocketbook. One of the burglars crept up and struck him on the back of the head with a crowbar. The lifeless policeman was still holding his pen, and the partial entry in his pocketbook was the last thing he ever did. As a result, training tweaked their instruction to: 'officers should write up their pocketbooks as soon as reasonably practicable.'

Sergeant Duxbury painfully explained criminal, traffic and public order offence definitions using acetate slides. The information was drip-fed, line by line. *Death by an Overhead Projector* was how the students referred to that particular method of instruction. Once we had mastered the offences, we moved on to the exemptions, legal defences and case law. There were always defences. For example, for religious reasons, a Sikh can wear a turban rather than a crash helmet when riding a motorbike. However, all the Sikhs I knew were intelligent enough to wear a helmet or buy a car.

Trainees spent evenings preparing our uniform for the morning inspections while reciting offence definitions, parrot-fashion, to revise for the Friday morning test.

The policewomen's accommodation block was strictly out of bounds to males, and the threatened punishment was instant dismissal. That threat only made the challenge more exciting for some. The path next to the ladies' block was called 'Passion Alley' - following the fortnightly disco, couples often embraced for a goodnight snog. If a lady shared her room number (and with twice the number of males compared to women, they could be choosy.) She might receive an early morning visit from her suitor, who may not have to use his knuckles to knock on her door. A 'Ryton Romance' was an aesthetically pleasing description for these dalliances. Rod Lee's view, "I heard they were at it like wildebeest in heat," was possibly more accurate.

With the number of students and some classes having only one trainer, it should have been easy to stay off the radar and slide through training unnoticed. However, some recruits cared not one jot about the radar. They included Dave, from the West Midlands, who used his room door for knife-throwing practice and nailed a bullwhip over his bed. The Camp Commandant invited Dave to his office and gave him a written warning.

Before a life-saving swimming lesson, two female students in full uniform stood by the pool. The instructor announced they had sore throats and would not be swimming. "What a load of bollocks," I said to Rod Lee, "I spoke to them this morning, and there's nothing wrong with their bloody throats."

"Vinnie, for fuck's sake, they're having their period. You know - on the blob." Though I never found out how Rod was privy to that information, I did learn a lot from him during the ten weeks.

On Wednesday afternoons, the entire college had a sports afternoon, which was shambolic. Rod and others proficient at rugby roughed up the recruits who misguidedly decided to take them on. I watched the rugby from the safety of a makeshift cross-country course. With his blond locks flowing, I could see Rod charging like a buffalo through a herd of traumatised probationers. It was carnage.

A tiny man taught self-defence. He was only ever referred to as *The Poison Dwarf,* so I cannot tell you his real name. He selected the frail and frightened to assist in demonstrating Home-Office approved self-defence and restraint techniques. Spitefully, he caused those he picked a little more pain and discomfort than necessary. Rod repeatedly volunteered to assist so he could dismantle the little fucker. However, the diminutive bully dismissed Rod with a wave of his tiny little hand.

A few weeks before my passing out parade, I collected a buff envelope marked 'Private and Personal' from the post room. "What's that, Smithy?" Rod Lee asked, "Is it your discharge papers? Fucking sacked before you have even started?" I shared the contents of the letter with my classmates.

"Because I was in the Army and worked for Redditch Council, they have transferred two and a half years into my police pension, which means I will retire in 2007. Whereas you lot will finish in 2009." I felt pretty sad at the time. However, in 2007, I was more than happy to bid farewell to the West Midlands Police.

As the class drill prefect, I marched my colleagues around the concourse. The inter-class drill competition was a keenly contested event. The night before the competition, the college Drill Sergeant said to me that my class had an excellent chance of winning, adding that the only thing which would stop us was my beard.

"What does my beard have to do with the drill comp, sarge?"

"I run the competition, and I won't be handing the winner's shield to some twat who can't even be bothered to get a shave. It's your choice, son." My beard had taken a while to grow, and I liked it. But my class had put a real effort into having a chance of winning. What should I do?

The following day, my class were ready to start the drill comp. "Squad Atten-Shun!" I shouted. I received a glare from the Drill Sergeant. We did not come even close to winning, but I kept my beard.

Those still involved with their *Ryton Romances* dissuaded partners from attending the passing out parade, trying to avoid a *Jerry Springer*-style confrontation to decide spousal ownership.

Following basic training, we all went our separate ways, and I only saw Rod Lee again socially. If we had worked together, I would probably have had to write my first book from our cell in Winson Green Prison.

Training completed, it was time to meet my new colleagues, and hope the British public would not tear me into little pieces before I knew what I was doing. I was twenty-three years old when I passed out from Ryton on Dunsmore.

Kings Heath police station added the probationer PC 8293, Vincent Smith, to their nominal role.

CHAPTER 3

THE HEATH OF KINGS

Kings Heath, the B3 Subdivision, was a brilliant place to learn my job. It had played a large part in Birmingham's history. The B3 was my imaginary island. I knew my colleagues but almost nothing about the neighbouring areas or the police officers who worked there. Here is a journey through Kings Heath, describing it as I could have in 1983 when I had three year's service.

"Ladies and gentlemen, you join me today on the number 50 bus at its terminus in Bells Lane, Druids Heath. This service runs every three minutes and is a main arterial route into Birmingham. When Birmingham's population exploded, from 70,000 in 1801 to 522,000 one hundred years later, Birmingham's suburbs developed at a remarkable pace."

"This route bisects the Kings Heath police subdivision. I am Police Constable 8293 Vince Smith, from the West Midlands police, your tour guide. Please remember smoking is only allowed upstairs."

Ding-Ding, we set off. "Right, ladies and gents, this is Druids Heath. You can see it is a council estate, with lots of high-rise flats. I overheard your comment, sir, and no, it is not an open prison. We are approaching the Maypole Island and will turn left onto the Alcester Road. West Mercia Police cover the area to the right. Directly opposite is the Maypole Inn, a pub built in the 1930s."

"We will stay on this road until we reach Birmingham. To your right, you can see The Horseshoe pub, built in 1883, adjacent to what was once a busy canal network. Again, on your right is Cocksmoor Woods, an 18-hole golf course that opened in 1926. Many, including Peter Allis, the golfer and television pundit, rate the course very highly. Continuing the journey, small parades of shops are on both sides of Alcester Road. On the left is the Kings Arms, built in 1795. As we continue, if you look to your right, you can see Kings Heath Squash and Cricket Club next to the Four Provinces Irish social club. At the junction with Wheelers Lane is King's Heaths Masonic Hall, built in 1936."

I fielded a question from one of the passengers, "No, sir, I am not a Freemason, because I have not been invited to join." By the way, I still haven't. "This is Kings Heath. In 1895, a young mother moved here from South Africa and set up home with her two young sons, Ronald and John Tolkien (Who is better known as JRR Tolkien the author of The Lord of the Rings). You can see the High Street with its bustling, vibrant shops which play host to some incredibly active shoplifters."

I continue: "The next pub on your left is the Hare and Hounds, built in 1826 and where, in 1979, the Moseley reggae/pop band UB 40 played their first gig. In 1983, they had their first number-one UK hit with *Red Red Wine*. On the left is the Cross Guns, built in 1826. The upstairs of the pub was a courtroom where the Justices of the Peace operated. Finally, towards the end of the parade of shops, on the left, is an Argos store. It is my favourite shop on the

High Street as they operate a pay-before-you-get-your-goods policy. A practice that meant they never had any shoplifters for me to deal with."

I continued, "If you look to the left, you can see Kings Heath Library, built in 1905, where I am a member. Right next to the library is Kings Heath police station, built in 1893. The Station pub, built in 1889, is directly opposite the police station. It refers not to the police station but to the Kings Heath train station, which has not operated since the 1960s."

"We are now approaching a small island. To your left, you can see Queensbridge Comprehensive School. After the island, on your right is Amblers Funeral Home, and on your left is The Reddings, the home of Moseley Rugby Football Club. They are one of the top rugby union clubs in England. It's also where my friend, Mark Linnet, a policeman in the West Midlands, made his debut in 1982."

"Crossing the traffic lights, we enter Moseley Village. In my opinion, it is the most bohemian suburb in Birmingham. Its residents include hippies, drug addicts, prostitutes, Members of Parliament, the homeless and UB 40. On the right is the Bulls Head, built in 1700 and the oldest pub on this route. The next pub, only separated from the Bulls Head by a Barclays Bank, a Travel-Agents and the Scientology Centre, stands the Fighting Cocks where on Boxing Day in 1759, a cockfighting competition took place between Warwickshire and Worcestershire. Each County entered fifteen cocks. The team that won the most cockfights received a cash prize of £10 - worth over £2,000 in 2024. I keep checking Teletext for the result of that contest without success. Cockfighting attracted visitors until it was outlawed in 1835."

"You might see a man wearing a cowboy hat with no shoes. His name is 'Pete the Feet.' He will be off to the Bulls Head to enjoy a pint of Old Speckled Hen. On your left and right are shops and restaurants." We journey on.

"On the right is the Prince of Wales pub, built in 1840. Before the First World War, to avoid being seen by his girlfriend's mother, who was also his landlady, JRR Tolkien regularly took his girlfriend to the smoke room at the back of the pub for a sneaky drink. Continuing the journey, on the left is the Regents Court pub, built in the 1960s."

"Ladies and Gents, we are now in Balsall Heath. Since the 1950s, this has been one of Birmingham's busiest vice areas. Prostitutes walk the streets or stand at junctions to attract clients. Cheddar Road is a short distance away. It is a cul-de-sac where prostitutes sit in the window, Amsterdam style, and ply their trade. Balsall Heath has some of the finest Asian restaurants in England. Its Victorian buildings include swimming baths, schools and the New Inn's pub. The last pub on this route before we leave the B3 area is the Castle and Falcon, built in 1852. Chris Stapleton became the licensee in the '80s and supplied Hughie McGowan and me with alcohol even when we were short of funds. The live music he played and arranged was fantastic as well."

"Ladies and Gents, that concludes our journey. I shall pass around my helmet and would be grateful if you would like to make a small donation."

Have you ever wondered why pubs have a large sign with a picture that depicts the pub's name? It's because when the pubs were built, most of the population was illiterate.

CHAPTER 4

LEARNING THE BASICS

When I arrived at Kings Heath police station, I spent three two-week stints with permanent beat officers based at Billesley, Woodbridge and Kings Heath.

Wearing spectacles at work made me feel vulnerable. Putting my glasses into my pocket before an altercation protected my spectacles but reduced my vision to a fuzzy blur, causing even more significant problems. I decided to wear contact lenses and persevered through the discomfort. It was January 1980. With my eyesight corrected, I joined my new crime-fighting amigos on B Unit.

My first shift was a 6am-2pm. I was excited and apprehensive as I cycled to work, ten cold miles, which took fifty minutes. During the journey, I reflected on my time in training. As we were all in the same boat, there was an element of camaraderie. Cycling to Kings Heath, I felt isolated and vulnerable and had no idea what to expect.

I arrived at 5.20am for a 5.45am shift parade. Sergeant Brian Roberts greeted me and steered me toward the kettle and B Unit's locker containing tea, coffee, sterilised milk, sugar and cups. The locker kept the contents safe from the thieves on the other shifts.

Muttering, "I don't even drink tea," Sergeant Roberts comforted me, "Well, that's one less brew you'll have to make then, son." As for sterilised milk, though loved by Brummies, it was awful stuff. It didn't taste, look or smell like milk and lasted years. At work, I occasionally had a black coffee. By not drinking tea, I avoided even an accidental encounter with sterilised milk.

I made fifteen cups of tea, filled a tray, and carried it into the parade room. My ungrateful shift accepted their brew as it was too late to remake it before the parade. At precisely 5.45am, Inspector Young, Sergeant Roberts, and Sergeant Mason entered the parade room. Roberts announced, "On Parade!"

Everyone put their hats on and stood up, and I followed suit. If they had all taken one shoe off and pushed a pencil up their nose, I would have, too. Constables presented their appointments - truncheons and handcuffs. The sergeants examined and signed officers' pocketbooks while Inspector Young confirmed the shift postings. Two Zulu vehicles - fast response cars - were double-crewed. Four Panda cars - single-crewed - were allocated according to the officer's length of service.

Officers assigned to front office duties had to be warned in advance as their start times were fifteen minutes ahead of the shifts. Sergeant Mason read out bulletin points from the station briefing book. I copied everyone else by making notes in my pocketbook.

Before I joined the police, my father gave me some advice. He told me never to worry about working with wankers as they would only make me look good. Secondly, never handcuff my wrist to a prisoner. Growing up in Belfast, he had seen a skinny policeman swung around by his handcuffed wrist like a helicopter's rotor blade. Dad described how the cop screamed in agony as his shoulder dislocated and extended the length of his arm by about a foot.

He imparted his final pearl of wisdom. I should leave my truncheon at the station. His rationale was, "Son, if you can't sort out a problem with your fists then, after receiving a bloody good hiding, your truncheon will probably be shoved straight up your arse." Wise words, Dad.

After the parade, rather than smearing it with lubricant, I put my truncheon in my locker for safekeeping. I carried my handcuffs on patrol but only used them on prisoners' wrists.

Colin Young, B Unit's shift Inspector, was a large, avuncular, experienced policeman. After the parade, Mr Young called me into his office for a two-minute chat. He told me the quality of my tea had better improve sharpish, or I would spend my entire probation making it. Also, his shift already had six probationers, and two more were on their way. He advised me to learn from the senior PCs and not to trouble the sergeants too much, as they had enough to do without wet nursing me. I was to write my prisoner and process offender's names in the back of my pocketbook, allowing my supervisors to see how busy I'd been.

As a posting that morning, I was to *Fly the Flag* - walk up and down the High Street and check that the shops were secure. "Only walk as far as Woolworths," Mr Young added, "then walk back. Do not go wandering. I could do without sending out a search party to find you on your first day." If Mr Young had known me better, he would have appreciated what a realistic possibility that was.

Armed with a Burndept police radio clipped to my tunic lapel, I hit the streets to meet the British public. I did a double-take the first time I saw my reflection in a shop window. Was that really me? I awkwardly walked the High Street, unsure at what speed to travel. I settled on quicker-than-a-shuffle without taking giant strides as if I were trying to flee the scene.

On the opposite side of the road from the police station was the Kingsway Cinema. Maybe if it was quiet on a late shift, I could stand at the back and watch a movie while I chatted with the usherette. It never happened. The cinema closed a few weeks later and became a Bingo hall. I didn't play bingo. In fact, I didn't take part in any blood sports.

I made eye contact with a young man at a bus stop and gave him a cheery "Good Morning." The lad, who looked anything but impressed, mockingly replied. "Christ, are you wearing that outfit for a bet? How much have you won?"

"Well, last time I checked my wage slip, it's about four and a half thousand pounds a year, plus overtime." PC 8293 Smith takes an early 1-0 lead.

The Police were at the top of the UK pop charts with their song, *Walking on the Moon.* The brand-new Doctor Martens boots I wore allowed a cushioned bounce. I was not exactly walking on the moon, but they were very comfortable.

The Kings Heath controller's office was on the ground floor and had a stable door entrance. The top half of the door was missing, allowing the controller to see officers as they walked to and from the adjacent report writing room. Line of sight was an even more effective way of dispatching resources than the police radio. The Inspector's office was adjacent, and instructions from the controller would be heard and supported by the gaffer.

Every job the police attended had a computer log. That log tagged officers to the incident. The controller contemporaneously made entries onto the log, including the officer's dispatch time, a summary of events, and the time officers cleared. Log printouts assisted the accuracy of the attending officer's pocketbook entry.

The report writing room, where the shift paraded, had a large table surrounded by a collection of chairs that looked like they had been purchased from a jumble sale. In the back corner of the room was a fire exit door. That exit facilitated the troops to starburst and attend urgent incidents. The room was a mess. There were four shifts, and each thought cleaning the parade room was another shift's responsibility. Ashtrays and empty cups were scattered everywhere. Three waist-high, narrow metal cabinets housed dozens of A4 police forms; every incident classification had a different form. Frustratingly, every drawer was incorrectly labelled. Some officers on my shift had cracked the code, so I had to ask or start searching.

Every submitted crime report included the name of the detective who had advised on its classification. Writing the name of a detective on the crime report without their knowledge was professional suicide.

The only item of equipment in the room was a typewriter, surrounded by sheets of carbon paper and, if you were lucky, an abandoned bottle of Tippex.

The typing skills of most police officers were non-existent. Officers coated the documents with so much Tippex they needed to be handled with care, as there was a distinct possibility that they could shatter if dropped.

Magistrate's case summaries required three copies. I learned never to leave a part-completed case summary in the typewriter unattended. Someone took the papers out of the typewriter and reversed the second sheet of carbon paper, which created a dog's dinner of a mess to sort out. Other stunts included sneakily scrolling up the form and typing near the bottom, "WANKERS", or worse, much worse.

My second day on the shift was another early, and for all the wrong reasons, I did not make the tea. After cycling for fifty minutes, I arrived at Kings Heath at 5.20am. I was wearing my army combat jacket as I had the day before.

Sergeant Brian Roberts was outside the nick and seemed to be waiting for someone. "Ah, it's our newest probationer, 'Wolfie Smith.' Did you enjoy your cycle ride to work this morning?" My camouflage jacket had triggered a shift discussion. I was dubbed 'Wolfie', after the lead character in the hit TV programme *Citizen Smith*. Brian Roberts was the least balanced of the four sergeants on my shift, prone to mood swings and facial twitches, "Yes, sarge, a bit cold, but no problem."

Sergeant Roberts was smiling, which was scary. "Listen, son, and I know this is only your second day on the shift. Has anyone enlightened you about your

ARD?" I had no idea what he was talking about and said so.

Roberts explained the twenty-eight-day police shift pattern to me. Twenty days were shifts, seven were fixed rest days, leaving one additional rest day, which floated across the shift pattern. I was confused. "Well, today is yours. So you can go home and get back into bed. I'll see you on Friday. It's another early, so don't be late." I set off with Robert's maniacal laughter ringing in my ears. He could have let me work my shift and take another day off, but where was the fun in that? I was angry and took it out on my pedals. I made it home in forty-five minutes.

A sergeant fielded paperwork submissions and examined every form with a fine-tooth comb. It was easy to tell which sergeant was on paperwork detail as they wore reading glasses, had furrowed brows and were at the end of their tether.

Apart from court papers, every other submission was handwritten. There was a lot of paperwork: statements, pocketbooks, sudden death forms, accident books, process books, crime reports, and supplementary crime reports. Recruits were at the bottom of a bloody steep learning curve. The critical lesson was not coping with the amount but prioritising what was important. The shift supervision knew that the faster probationers shaped up, the easier their job would become, so they allowed us no wiggle room.

No matter what anyone thinks, there were no extra-curricular courses teaching racism, sexism, how to assault prisoners or the dark art of stitching up criminals.

Length of service defined the pecking order on the shift. When overtime or courses became available, supervision selected the nominees. Taking the piss out of a sergeant was not a smart move. It resulted in a straight to the back of the queue for everything punishment.

Due to their limited availability, driving course allocation often resulted in cheers, tears or tantrums. I watched with impunity as I didn't even hold a driving licence - the minimum requirement to attend a driving course.

When an alarm activated, resources headed towards the attacked premises. Then, one of the more experienced, usually the Zulu observer, would shout out escape routes that needed to be covered by the attending vehicles. It was impressive and effective.

Learning how to document prisoners could have been a long, slow process. However, the High Street had plenty of shops, which meant it had shoplifters a'plenty. I had the pleasure of arresting most of them during my time at Kings Heath. A shoplifter's interview, documentation and charge took four hours. The forms, charge sheets, and court papers became second nature through repetition. Antecedent forms and fingerprints were examined and signed by the custody sergeant. All prisoners required two sets of their fingerprints to be taken. If a prisoner resisted, what should have been a ten-minute task could take an hour. Prisoners had to be processed for every arrest as their fingerprints proved the detainee's identity.

While fingerprinting a prisoner in the documentation room, PC Barry Melvin, a colossal specimen, brought in his prisoner. Barry's chest hair sprouted over his collar, attempting to merge with his beard. Barry spoke slowly, with a strong possibility that the repeated use of steroids had fuddled his brain.

On Barry's shift was a lad called Stevie Marshall, who, at nine stone wringing wet, risked his life by tormenting Barry. One night, Barry fell into a deep sleep during their refreshment break. Stevie tied Barry's shoelaces together and had the controller shout on the radio, "Officer Requires Urgent Assistance!" Barry sprang off his chair, his laces prevented him from getting far, and he collapsed in a heap, muttering, "I'm going to fucking kill you, Marshall."

Another incident, orchestrated by Steve Marshall, had the Inspector brief Barry, 'The SAS will arrive by helicopter in Kings Heath Park for a top-secret mission.' He showed Barry how to hold two torches and cross the beams so the pilot could see where to land. At 4am, Barry stood alone in the middle of the park. The shift knew what was happening. After twenty minutes, Melvin radioed in. The radio was on talk-through, which meant the shift could hear his transmission. "PC Melvin, to control, are you receiving?" A collective sigh of disappointment fizzed around the shift. Had Barry worked out that this was yet another prank? "Bravo three control PC Melvin, go ahead."

"Sarge, one of my torches needs a battery. Can you get someone to drop one off as soon as possible? I think I can hear the helicopter approaching." At 5am, Barry realised he had again been the victim of a wind-up. The controller sensibly sent someone other than Steve Marshall to retrieve Barry.

Back in the fingerprint room at Kings Heath, Barry's prisoner had realised that PC Melvin was not this year's BBC Mastermind champion. Barry sensed his contempt, "Right, son, I've got to fill this in," he held up the pink four-page antecedence booklet, "so no fucking about, okay." The prisoner shrugged. Barry continued, "Right, question one, what is your full name in block capitals?" I spat out my coffee. Barry's prisoner shook his head and said to me, "Is there something actually wrong with him?" Then, as steam started to come out of Barry's ears, I returned my prisoner to the safety of his cell.

In 1980, non-UK residents charged with a criminal offence also received a deportation notice. Following conviction, expulsion was a sentencing option. It seemed more of an administrative issue, given the severity of the crimes I was dealing with - shoplifting, shoplifting, and did I mention shoplifting?

While I was in the parade room, writing up my pocketbook, the paperwork sergeant examined the shift's submissions in the inspector's office. I was waiting to see if my work would be signed and passed up the chain of command or rejected and returned.

Sergeant Mason walked into the parade room holding a crime report and its attached papers. It was my crime report. It was possible, but very unlikely, that he was about to tell me that I had been awarded a gold star for effort. "Wolfie, is this your crime report?" As my name, collar number and signature were written on the first fifteen pages of the bundle, a denial would have been ludicrous.

"Yes, sarge, is there a problem?" It looked like there was,

"I am not sure if you would consider it to be a problem, but I have read the first four pages of your supplementary crime report, and I must say, while I am very interested in purchasing the film rights, I have to ask, on what page have you written anything relating to the circumstances of the offence?"

"Okay, sarge, I will do it again and resubmit it." Sergeant Mason frisbeed the bundle in my direction and warned, "Oh, and if that cluster of bollocks requires more than a one-page supplementary, then you are probably in the wrong fucking job."

As panda cars needed to be kept free to respond to emergencies, the controller tracked down probationers and had a patrol car collect and transport them to meet Kings Heath's latest shoplifter. Which was how I met Seamus in Woolworths on the High Street. He was a chirpy young lad from Dublin. Seamus had exited Woolworths without offering payment for the curtains he had hidden under his jacket. An eagle-eyed store detective detained him and contacted the police. It was not his first arrest.

During his interview, Seamus made a full and frank admission. After which, he made me a nice cup of black coffee. What a lovely chap.

When I charged Seamus with shoplifting as a Citizen of Eire, I served him with a deportation notice. The custody sergeant bailed him to appear before the Birmingham Magistrates in three weeks. Before he left the station, Seamus asked what I thought would happen to him at court. Drawing on my non-existent experience, "For a guilty plea, you will possibly get probation." As he was leaving, I called out, "Hey, Seamus. I know you don't have the curtains anymore but isn't it about time you pulled yourself together." We laughed.

Three weeks later, while at the Magistrates Court. I went to court two and saw a smiling Seamus bounce into the dock. I nodded in response to the blatant thumbs-up he greeted me with. Maybe we could go for a pint after his release and discuss how funny my 'pull yourself together' comment was.

The Chairman of the Magistrates had a pinched face and wore his spectacles perched on the end of his nose. He looked like a Victorian headmaster about to deal with a problem pupil.

The Prosecuting Solicitor outlined the circumstances of the offence. Seamus pleaded guilty to a single charge of theft, shops and stalls, contrary to the Theft Act of 1968. The Chairman of the Magistrates snootily peered over his glasses and addressed Seamus, "Young man, stand up straight and wipe that stupid grin off your face." I feared the worst but was relieved the death penalty was not an option. Sneering at Seamus and enjoying every second, he continued. "I am sentencing you to six months imprisonment. Following which, you will be deported to the Irish Republic. Sergeant, please take him away."

Seamus was shocked, so I avoided the - '*But you said*' look that he fired at me. After that, I never guessed what would happen in court again.

CHAPTER 5

ANOTHER ONE BITES THE DUST

My son Peter was born in May 1980, and proud though I was, my life had become a lot busier. The shifts were hard work and long hours. Nights were Monday to Sunday, 10pm-6am, and they came around far too frequently. The fifty-minute bike ride to work was not helping either.
My civilian friends complained that I was either on nights, coming off nights or about to start nights, and we drifted apart.

I used my Police Federation diary to jot down a year's commitments - shifts, court, courses, leave, and not forgetting my monthly ARD. I carried the diary in my rear trouser pocket for access and reference.

Because of Maggie's generous pay rise, police officers vacated police authority accommodation and bought their own houses. Police houses were rent and rates free but purchasing a house qualified officers for a substantial tax-free rent allowance. A police house anywhere in Birmingham would assist me greatly.

I asked a housing clerk at police headquarters for the details of any available police houses. He scrolled through his records, and I hit *pay dirt*. A three-bedroomed terraced house in Sunderton Road, Kings Heath, was empty.

The décor and condition of a police house was potluck. Some were vacated in pristine condition and left with carpets and curtains. Others looked like the occupants had neglected them for years and only left when they were no longer habitable. 178 Sunderton Road was in a block of four police houses, and the location was perfect. I needed to assess it before agreeing to move my family in. Sunderton Road was near the main Alcester Road on the 50-bus route - an absolute godsend for someone without a car based at Kings Heath police station. I decided to check it out straight away.

As I walked up the path, I heard a noise coming from inside the house. It was time to introduce myself to the local ne'er do wells. I burst in and saw two men on the stairs. Both were policemen who worked at Kings Heath police station. "What the hell do you think you're doing?" My question was redundant as they were ripping out the stair carpet. One blurted, "It's Wolfie Smith, isn't it? All right, mate, we're your new neighbours, and we weren't sure if you wanted to keep the carpets, so we were removing them for you. Okay?"

I could see an open window in the kitchen. "Actually, gents, everything is pretty far from okay. Leave the carpet where it is and go. Oh, and leave through the front door, as it'll save you clambering through the kitchen window again." Contritely, well, I had caught them committing an offence of burglary; one of them said, "Wolfie, that's fair enough, but if you ever need anything, you only have to ask."

"Gents, I will keep the carpets, curtains and the stone fireplace. Don't break in again, or I will invite another police officer to attend, one on duty and in uniform." Within two weeks, I had moved into Sunderton Road.

My Inspector Colin Young did not accept anything at face value, and whenever he challenged me, I crumbled. Once, my pathetic excuse for being late was fixing a bogus puncture on my bike. He held my hand and inspected it. With no corroborative dirt or oil, he sighed and said, "Really?" I never misled him again to avoid being nicknamed 'Billy Liar' for the remainder of my career.

Shift sergeants had supervisory responsibility and were highly suspicious of all recruits. After a first-watch parade, Sergeant Roberts handed me a summons to serve at 42 Nafford Grove, near the Maypole.

I had forgotten all about the summons. At 1.25pm, I was in the station, killing time before going off duty. Sergeant Roberts asked for an update about the summons. I rather stupidly said I had been to the address but could not get a reply. Roberts twitchily eyed me up and down. "So, what colour is the front door of number 42 Nafford Grove?"

"I'll be back as quick as I can, sarge."

"PC Smith, you are about as useful as an unfinished wank." I didn't enjoy being insulted, but the originality of his line made it easier to accept.

Using the number 50 bus, I made a thirty-minute round trip to the Maypole and back. I served the summons. It was 2pm, and disappointedly, Roberts was still at work. He put his hand out, and I gave him a copy of the served summons. He hadn't finished with me, "So, what colour was the front door?"

"It was red. I apologise, sarge, and it will never happen again." He had made his point, and I never forgot it. He mellowed, "Wolfie, lesson learned. I have put the tea makings away. Wash the cups, and then you can get off."

Being the new kid on the shift put the onus on me, and I tried to fit in somewhere between everyone's new best friend and being a decent bloke. Making the tea counted for nothing, as everyone knew teamakers only acted out of duty.

Being a probationer meant any job could land in my lap. I approached every incident with the same level of naivety. I watched the 'old sweats' become invisible - 'The scene of a fatal road traffic accident needs guarding for the rest of the shift' (In the pouring rain.) Or don a high visibility jacket to catch Gaffer's eye for - 'Two days weekly leave are available for this weekend, any takers?"

While B Unit was on duty, I felt comfortable. If I popped into the station when B Unit was on a rest day, it was the same building with officers I didn't know. I felt almost unwelcome. Same furniture and fittings but different chemistry and conduct.

Socially, after lates, the shift had a beer at the Station pub, allowing issues that may have gnawed away for months to be resolved over a beverage. After one 2-10, B Unit gathered in the lounge. Ian Rollason sought out Dave Wilcox, "Wilco, I was in the Fighting Cocks earlier and shouted for backup. Everyone else turned up, so where the hell were you?"

"Sorry Rollo, I was down Waldrons Moor, chasing one of the Benson family who I thought was disqualified from driving. Unfortunately, I stopped the only member of that tribe who could drive legally on the road. I had no reception on my radio. By the time I reconnected, I knew there had been a problem, but the controller told me you had sorted it."

Sergeant Brian Lewis, the controller, was close enough to hear Rollo's challenge and nodded to confirm Wilco's account. Everyone, including the local criminals, knew Waldrons Moor was a police radio black spot. Rollo bought Wilco a lager. Matter sorted.

I worked a late with Ian Rollason. He trawled the sub-division looking for miscreants. I saw a flash and heard a thud as something hit a wooden advertising board. A teenager ran off. I told Rollo what I had seen. I can't call it a chase, as Rollo captured the lad in seconds. The advertising board had two Chinese death stars embedded in it. We took the Kung Fu kid to the nick. On the way, he asked, "If I admit it, can I have my stars back? They cost me a fiver."

Two probationers joined the shift six weeks after I started and took over the tea-making duties. One was Dave Shaw, who had an incredible career and retired as the Chief Constable of West Mercia. I enjoyed working with Dave - he looked so young, but he knew his stuff. Whenever Dave made decisions at an incident, the member of the public he spoke to would look past Dave and ask me if he was right. I confirmed he was because, unlike me, he knew the law.

Years later, Dave was an Assistant Chief Constable working at Lloyd House. He called me into his office, and we had a chat. I saw on his wall a small framed certificate. It was a sports day award from Tritiford Junior School in Kings Heath. Dave had achieved third place in the long jump. He told me that if he had finished first or second, he would not have had the certificate framed and mounted as it would have been boastful. That was typical of him.

At 8am, on a first watch, Mr Young called me into his office. He referred to a Midlands Regional Crime Intelligence (MRCI) circulation sheet and told me that over the previous month, a gang of men had entered supermarkets; while one caused a distraction by screaming and attacking stacked displays, others targeted the tills, stealing as much cash as possible. The gang had successfully stolen thousands of pounds. My role was to inform the store managers to make their staff aware.

Two days later, at 10am, the manager at Safeways supermarket, High Street, Kings Heath, rang 999 and reported that a robbery was in progress. I heard Yankee Mike broadcast the call and ran across the road to the premises. I thought, wow, those MRCI officers really knew their stuff.

I was one of the first to arrive, and the manager, whom I had met a few days before greeted me, "Officer, it was like you said. Come this way," I followed him down an aisle. I saw the staff lying across their tills to deter any would-be robbers. Halfway down the frozen food aisle, prostrate on the floor, was a tall Rastafarian man. He was wearing a large knitted red, yellow and green Rasta hat. The dreadlocks, not gathered by his hat, hung free. The man was motionless and surrounded by tins of baked beans.

"Officer, he walked around the store, screamed, fell to the ground and demolished a massive display of Heinz baked beans. (Other brands were available.) I shouted, 'Protect the tills' and dialled 999." The man on the floor had not moved.

I dropped to my haunches and started checking for vital signs. I removed the large Rasta hat and started laughing. I could see what the problem was. On top of his dreadlocks, there was a large frozen chicken. He was not part of a sophisticated team of robbers but a shoplifter who had made a very poor choice of *modus operandi*. A cup of tea resolved his physical problems. The manager banned him from the store but allowed him to keep the chicken.

In May 1980, Inspector Young became the General Duties Inspector. His replacement was pedantic and determined to stamp his authority on the shift. I thought he had possibly been potty trained at gunpoint as a child.

Phil Arnold, who joined the shift with Dave Shaw, was a lovely lad who tried hard but had no luck. If the shift swooped and arrested three burglars, Phil's prisoner would be a refused charge with complications. Phil once stopped a car for a routine check. The driver was a miffed Superintendent from Lloyd House. Phil had a sort of reverse *Midas touch*. Repeated meetings with our Inspector, who pointed out everything Phil was doing wrong, did little for his confidence.

PC John William Jones turned up on B Unit. I looked up to John. He was 6' 4", so I had no choice. John sustained a severe back injury while chasing a burglar. John jumped over a three-foot wall, unaware of a twelve-foot drop on the other side. He landed in a heap and was off work for months. Following his recovery, he joined B Unit Kings Heath.

The Inspector briefed John about the 'Phil Arnold situation.' He posted John and Phil to patrol the High Street for a week of nights. So that John could assess Phil without the distraction of rushing around in a panda car.

When John Jones worked nights, he looked impressive. Wearing his police helmet, he stood almost seven feet tall. John wore an old-fashioned police cape with a chain fastened at the neck. While he looked like a policeman from the 1880s, his street craft was pure 1980s. John and Phil patrolled the High Street and had prisoners every night. By anyone's standards, that was impressive. After the last night shift, John Jones spoke to the Inspector.

John mistakenly thought the Inspector had seen enough to realise that Phil would make an excellent police officer if given the chance. Sadly not, the Inspector had decided to sack Phil, and it was no longer a matter for discussion. Annoyed and frustrated, John felt he had wasted a week on a fool's errand. John loudly argued Phil's case, and we could hear him from the parade room. John's parting shot was that the Inspector only wanted his 'I've dismissed a probationer box' to be ticked. John slammed the door on his way out.

The West Midlands Police formally dispensed with Phil Arnold's services.

Note: A few months later, I saw Phil Arnold's name on the front page of the Birmingham Evening Mail. While working nights for a security firm at the Bull Ring shopping centre, Phil arrested three burglars breaking into shops. The trial judge commended Phil for his bravery. However, to this day, John Jones still feels annoyed about Phil Arnold's dismissal.

My new Inspector was a strange fish. On nights, he posted a policeman to join him in the police canteen, and they played *Space Invaders* all night. On another occasion, he dressed as an old lady and used himself as bait for street muggers. Maybe the West Midlands Police should have kept Phil Arnold and dispensed with my Inspector's services.

I attended courses at Bournville Lane. They built on and developed skills I had learned during initial training and on the streets. My little brother hated my self-defence and restraints courses as I practised them on him when I got home. Anthony disliked the *chicken wing* restraint, folding the wrist while firmly holding the thumb to control a prisoner. But, through his pain, my technique drastically improved.

My brother coped with a lot for the six years I was away in the Army. He developed an encyclopaedic knowledge of football. How well does he know his football? Years later, while staying in a hotel, my brother met the footballer Steve Nicol, who played for Liverpool during their heyday in the 1980s. Steve was chatting about his career, matches, goals and transfer fees. My brother had to correct the Scottish international on almost everything he remembered. Steve Nichol quickly realised my brother was far more qualified to write his biography than he was. A man who had been at the bar noticed Steve Nicol and loudly said,

"Stevie Nicol, my man... me and my mates were discussing the 1984 European Cup Final. After you blasted the first penalty over the bar in the penalty shoot-out, who took and scored Liverpool's second penalty?" Steve, probably a little pissed off at being reminded about possibly the worst moment of his career, took a sip of his drink and said, "Ask him," and pointed to my brother. The man who asked the question looked quizzically at Anthony. "That was Phil Neal, mate, and Liverpool won the shoot-out 4-2." Steve Nicol nodded and smiled.

Maybe it was a coping mechanism. Mentioning any family event will trigger my brother's memory with the details of a football match, the score and a reasonable attendance estimate.

The shift was a fluid group of individuals with lots of personnel coming and going. Officers often left or arrived without an explanation. Others went on promotion, retirement, or because management shuffled officers to balance the skills across the four shifts.

Mick Disney was a panda driver on B Unit, and we became friends. Mick had grey hair and a dark beard. His pipe was more of a 'Sherlock Holmes' prop than something he used for smoking. After a few weeks,

Mick talked me into joining the Birmingham 'Go' Society.

On Wednesday evenings, shifts permitting, we travelled to Birmingham and spent a couple of hours playing 'Go'. It is a game that takes a minute to learn but a lifetime to master and is played on a board divided into 324 squares. Opponents, in turn, use black and white pebbles to occupy the intersections to claim territory and capture pieces. 'Go' dates back to 450AD when Attila the Hun spent the day slaughtering his enemies, then rushed home for a game of 'Go' and a cup of cocoa - I made the cocoa bit up. Mick, who was far too nice to be a policeman, left and returned to his previous job.

After a late shift, John Rees, Caroline Sweeney and I decided to move upmarket and have a beer at the Oxford Hotel in Moseley. We wore jackets over our uniform. I ordered three pints of lager, and the service was excellent. However, the cigarette butts floating in our drinks were not quite so impressive. I sent the lager back and refused to pay. I learnt that not all establishments were pro-police. John drove us to the Station pub where the gaffer, Peter Padaruski, could be techy, but at least he kept his lager nicotine-free.

On the last shift of a week of nights, I attended a burglary at a house near the Maypole. It was shortly after midnight. The husband and wife recognised the offender as he climbed out of their kitchen window, carrying a stolen purse. They named him and said he had broken into their house before.

Officers searched the area without success. A PNC check confirmed the suspect's address. Then, with five officers in two panda cars, we set off to make an arrest.

Arriving at the house, two officers went to the rear in case the suspect tried to escape. I knocked on the front door, which opened immediately.

"Good morning. Sorry about the time, but we have to speak to your son Danny. Is he in?"

"He's not in. You bastards blame him for everything. Why can't you leave him alone?"

"Would you mind if we have a look?"

"Help yourselves, you normally do."

Three of us went in. It was a tiny house. I said to the lady,

"We need to check upstairs."

"There are two bedrooms; the smaller one is Danny's. Jim, go with them."

It turned out that Jim was Danny's stepdad. As soon as we were upstairs, Jim put his fingers to his lips, called me into the small bedroom and quietly said,

"Right, you are after that thieving fucker that lives here. Danny came home, packed his tent, and fucked off on his motorbike, which is neither taxed nor insured."

"Do you know where he is?"

"He has gone to one of his six Aunts, the wife's sisters. There is nowhere else he can go. While you were speaking to my missus, I ripped this sheet out of our phone contact's book. Here are their addresses and phone numbers. Sorry, but they are all over Birmingham. Find the bastard, lock him up and throw away the key. I have to go downstairs now, or she will get suspicious." I pocketed the scrap of paper and followed Jim downstairs. I said to the lady of the house,

"Thank you for your co-operation. We will be off now."

Keeping up his pretence, Jim called us a bunch of wankers as we left.

We headed back to Kings Heath, and I spoke to my Inspector. I told him I believed the information was genuine - the list of Aunties, addresses and phone numbers was far too elaborate to be a wind-up. He pondered for a minute and said,

"Okay, it's pretty quiet. Take two panda cars and six officers. Plan your route and bring me back a burglar. Please update me through the night. Good luck."

I gave Dave Wilcox the list of addresses, and in seconds, he worked out a route, and then we set off. On our journey, I saw parts of Birmingham that I had never seen before, or since, for that matter. Having updated the Inspector after every failure, he authorised his posse of deputies to continue.

It was 6.15am when we arrived at the last address. As I walked up the path, I saw a motorbike on the lawn, which was promising. The front door opened, and Danny, carrying a crash helmet and wearing a well-packed rucksack, walked into the welcoming arms of the law, namely me.

On the way to Kings Heath's custody suite, Danny said we were lucky, as he was off to live rough in the woods, and we would never have found him. I wrote out my arrest statement and left Danny to be dealt with by the CID.

I heard nothing for weeks, then on Divisional orders, I saw that Danny had admitted 112 burglary offences to a detective. I received a commendation for the arrest.

Having completed her two-year probation, Caroline Sweeney decided it was time to pick grapes in France and resigned from the police.

She still disputes my recollection of her actions at a disturbance in the Lion and Lamb pub in Balsall Heath. I was one of three officers who followed Caroline as she flew into the bar. A half dozen drunken Irishmen were squaring up to each other. They were determined to resolve issues that had festered for hundreds of years - The Battle of the Boyne and the Irish potato famine, to name only two. Caroline started kicking the men's shins. The fighting never started as those bitter old men had to sit down and rub their legs. It wasn't Home Office approved but bloody effective, nonetheless.

Caroline, when the fighting Irish from Balsall Heath found out you had left the police, they stopped wearing shin pads on their nights out. True story.

Barry Melvin decided he required a job where lifting heavy things was the only skill he would ever need. He handed in his uniform and left. Stevie Marshall took his giant metal Maglite torch, which was almost the same size as him, and transferred to the Greater Manchester Police. Possibly to search for some other colossus to torment. Hang on, wasn't 'Giant Haystacks' the wrestler from Manchester? I missed Phil, Mick, Caroline and Steve.

Absences allowed officers on overtime to fill in. One morning, I was posted to Zulu 7. A graded driver from A Unit whom I had only ever seen in passing introduced himself,

"Ah, it's Wolfie Smith, isn't it? I don't suppose your cycling proficiency badge allows you to drive the Zulu. So, I will be behind the wheel today. You better have this." He handed me a bog-standard black bic ballpoint pen. "Jack, I have a pen. Why would I need yours?"

"That's because you will be doing all the writing today, and I do mean <u>all</u> the writing."

Jack laughed, which sounded like the noise a donkey would make if you put a piping hot potato up its arse.

A family woke up and discovered someone had broken into their house and stolen their television. They reported the break-in to the police. The controller dispatched BZ7. On route, Jack chuntered,

"This is not a job for the Zulu. What are all the panda drivers doing? I've got somewhere I need to be in a bit."

We arrived at the burgled house at 7.30am. My initial assessment was that a crime report and two witness statements were required. I sat down, opened my folder and took out the necessary forms. Jack decided it was time to make his exit, "Right then, Wolfie, I will leave it with you. I am going to do that thing I told you about earlier. I will come back in an hour or so. I'm on the radio if you need me." Jack left.

I was finishing the second statement when Jack returned. Though I wasn't a detective, the egg yolk and tomato sauce on his shirt indicated that he had been stuffing his face while I had been busy. Jack imperiously walked into the lounge and radioed the controller,

"Bravo Zulu 7 to Control, can you put this address down for a visit by a Scenes of Crime Officer?"

"B3 Control to Bravo Zulu 7, I already have Jack. Wolfie requested SOCO at 8.30am after he had finished the house-to-house enquiries."

The guy I was taking a statement from quietly said, "How would you manage without him?"

To add insult to injury, when we arrived at Kings Heath for our grub break, Jack said he wasn't that hungry and asked if I fancied a game of snooker. I ordered a breakfast and waited in the canteen.

In August 1980, at 2pm, I was on uniform foot patrol on the High Street. As I approached Silver Street, I saw a red Ford Sierra parked on the pavement, across the junction and on double yellow lines. I thought - could the driver be carrying out a robbery at the adjacent Nat West bank? I looked into the bank and saw several customers, but none wore a balaclava or were toting a firearm.

I issued a parking ticket for the double yellow line offence and tucked it under the car's windscreen wiper. I was about to resume patrol when an angry man charged out of the bank and shouted, "What on earth are you bloody doing?" He looked like a businessman in his early fifties, wearing glasses and carrying a briefcase.

Confirming the car was his, I pointed out the three offences. I explained that I had only given him a parking ticket for the double yellow line offence. Rather than appease, it seemed to make things worse.

He declared, "I thought a paperclip was the oracle." I had no idea what he was talking about and said so.

"Look here, you knob. It's as plain as the nose on your face!" He pointed to a paperclip which sat snugly inside the tax disc holder. I explained that I had not long come out of training, but the 'paperclip defence' had not featured. He put the parking ticket in his pocket. He said he was going to make a formal complaint about me.

At 5pm, I walked into the nick to take my refreshment break. Sergeant Cliff Doughty was in the front office. He saw me and started laughing, "Wolfie, I might have guessed he was talking about you."

Cliff called me into a room behind the front office and explained. While he was angry when he left me, the man I had ticketed was ready to explode when he marched into the nick. He was insistent the uniformed clown he had met on the High Street needed sacking. Cliff listened to his rant for five minutes, then invited him into the station to lodge his complaint in the Official Police Complaints Office - there isn't one. Cliff led the chuntering man along a corridor, opened a door and gestured for the chap to enter. Once inside, Clang! Cliff closed and locked the cell door.

When the man calmed down, Sergeant Doughty charged him with disorderly conduct in a police station. Cliff explained the 'paperclip defence' to me. A beat officer responsible for the High Street, told a few shop owners that if they were just banking their takings, to place a paperclip in their tax disc holder, and he wouldn't issue a parking ticket. Who knew?

The BBC News reported that Mark Chapman had shot and killed John Lennon on a street in New York. Lennon was only forty years old. I liked The Beatles, but I loved the musical talent and sharp wit of John Lennon. I was gutted. *Imagine* was John Lennon's second solo album and the first I bought as a kid. Lennon is also responsible for my favourite quote,
"Everything will be okay in the end. If it's not okay, it's not the end.
RIP John Lennon, 8 December 1980.

CHAPTER 6

NOW AND THEN

When a defendant entered a not-guilty plea at the magistrate's court, it was time to get busy. Crown court trials required a committal file that included a neatly typed - case summary, witness statements, a witness list and an exhibit list. The Prosecuting Solicitors (Now CPS) memo usually had a request for the OIC to conduct further enquiries. The additional work was disparagingly referred to by officers as "I think he has sent me his fucking shopping list."

Pros Sols knew a polite message would be a waste of time, so even the first request contained threats of case dismissal. It was time to try to get Barbara Cartland, the Kings Heath typist, on board. 'Babs' had her favourites, Milk Tray, Roses and Quality Street, to name only three.

A light shone at the end of a long, dark paperwork tunnel - small carbonated forms sufficed to report criminal damage valued at £20 or less. A standard white report could suffice for other incidents, providing that you could explain that it was unclear what, or indeed if anything, had occurred. An Inspector could file the report as 'no crime.' This was not a course of action recommended to mere probationers.

Eventually, the West Midlands police filed so many 'no crime' reports Her Majesty's Inspectorate of Constabulary intervened. They instructed that all 'no crimes' were converted into crime reports.

Preventing my force from masking their <u>actual</u> crime figures.

The 'masters of work avoidance' had another option, the Minor Occurrence Book. With scant details and by being economical with the truth, an officer could file an incident in the station MOB. The entry always concluded, 'All parties have been advised regarding their future conduct and are completely satisfied with the actions of the police.' The reporting officer did not highlight - the disparity in ages, weapons or the extent of injuries.

Experienced officers would return to the scene and ensure there had been no further flare-ups before committing pen to pocketbook and MOB. The creative effort put into these entries had to be seen to be appreciated.

Shift Inspectors visited police stations to check and sign the MOB. They paid more attention to the author than the incident. Legend has it that murders found their way into the Minor Occurrence Book before further scrutiny resulted in full-blown murder inquiries.

At 11am, I collected a bag of exhibits from the property officer at Kings Heath. The Prosecuting Solicitor in Court 2 at the Magistrates Court required the exhibits for a trial starting at 2pm.

Shortly after midday, I quietly entered Court 2. A trial was in full flow, so I sat in the public gallery and waited. The six Irishmen in the dock looked like casualties from a battlefield - head wounds, broken limbs, crutches and blood-stained bandages. The

Stipendiary (A legally qualified magistrate) summed up the previous night's debacle.

"Gentlemen, your behaviour in the Lion and Lamb public house last night was disgraceful. You were all, quite rightly, arrested for causing an affray. A number of you have sustained serious injuries."

I couldn't help but think that if Caroline Sweeney had remained in the police and attended the incident, the defendants would have avoided a court appearance and been at home, nursing very sore shins.

"However, you have all decided not to make any statements of complaint. You appear to be known to each other, and your issues have festered for years." He paused to allow this to sink in, and those who could nod did so. Then he continued, "I have decided to bind you over to be of good behaviour for the next twelve months." Those defendants who were unable to nod smiled. The Stipendiary delivered what he thought was a knockout blow. "Your bind over will be conditional. I believe alcohol is the root of your problem, so the condition of your bind-over will be that you do not drink alcohol for the next twelve months." That wiped the smiles off the faces of the defendants. Maybe he should have left it there. "And when I say no alcohol, I include even the smallest glass of sherry before your evening meal."

The Irishmen left the courtroom, and confident that the judge would not be following them headed towards the nearest boozer.

When I joined, if a concerned person called the police to report noises coming from a neighbour's house, irritated officers, who thought they had much better things to do, responded and here is a typical update.

"Bravo Mike Two Zero, to control. Can I update the log about the so-called disturbance at 243 Church Road, Moseley?"

"Bravo Three Control, go ahead, Jim."

"Okay, in a nutshell. Bill was late getting home from work, and his missus had cremated his dinner by leaving it under the grill. So far?"

"Bravo Three received so far."

"Following an exchange of words, it all got a bit animated. I have advised Jim's wife to sort out her cooking. I have also told Bill to keep his hands to himself. Because if I have to return, he will get bounced off the walls in his living room like a squash ball."

"Bravo Three received so far."

"Write this off as a 'Domestic Dispute'. If the nosey neighbour rings the police again, tell her to draw her curtains and turn up the volume on her television. I will float past on my travels if I get the chance." Delivering the message piecemeal allowed the controller to update the police log contemporaneously.

As an assessment, 'a domestic dispute' confused rather than clarified. It masked two critical questions – is there a victim?- is there an offender? A description of the same incident could have included - domestic violence, family violence or spousal abuse. Note - the officer's update did not include history, allegations, fears, concerns, injuries or children because that would only complicate matters.

It took a long time, but when the police realised 'domestic disputes', unchecked, often escalated into 'domestic murders', it was time to take action. Protocols and procedures drastically changed. Though not perfect, the quality of service offered now is unrecognisable from the ten-minute approach of the 1980s.

Police interviews of victims, witnesses or suspects took place in any room in the station. If an officer interviewed a suspect for an hour, they might write fifteen pages of interview notes in their pocketbook. Months later, at the Crown Court, having confirmed under oath, they had recorded every word of the interview. They read out their pocket notebook entry; that took seven minutes, so being asked to account for the remaining fifty-three minutes was a problem.

A Derby detective, whom I admire for his bravery and stupidity, gave evidence at Crown Court. His interview with the defendant was critical to the case. The detective had read twenty-five pages of that interview to the court. Everything was going thunderingly well. The defence barrister interrupted the detective's evidence and addressed the judge.

"My Lord, could I examine this officer's pocketbook, as something does not seem quite right?"

"Of course. Officer, hand your pocketbook to the court usher." The detective baulked at the request and appealed to the judge, "I would rather not, sir. My pocketbook contains details of a highly sensitive nature."

"Detective, hand over your pocketbook. Now!"

The usher had to tug the pocketbook from the detective's hand and passed it to the defence barrister. The barrister sat down and theatrically turned the pages of the notebook. After a couple of minutes, the barrister stood up to address the judge.

"My Lord, I will deal first with the detective's concerns. There is nothing of a highly sensitive nature in his pocketbook." The judge queried, "Are you sure?"

"I am, and the reason that I am is that this pocketbook does not contain a single written word." For effect, he flicked through the blank pages while holding up the pocketbook. While the detective sweated profusely in the witness box. The judge dismissed the case.

A red-faced Superintendent stood on the crown court steps at the hastily arranged press conference. In due course, he promised the officer would be 'Struck down with great vengeance and furious anger,' or words to that effect.

Police officers writing prisoner interviews contemporaneously, was that foolproof? Not really. If a prisoner did not sign the notes, which was often the case, their creation date could not be provenanced. Finally, the 1984 Police and Criminal Evidence Act ordered that interviews were tape-recorded, secured and retained.

Commendations are how the police reward officers for outstanding work. I received my first in 1980 for the off-duty arrest of two youths that Johnny Mac and I caught syphoning petrol out of a car. Senior officers liked their staff making off-duty arrests, so the impressive phrase 'Dedication to Duty' could be used on the commendation certificate. I received twenty-three commendations during my career with the West Midlands police and have retained a few for posterity.

My favourites include one from my Chief Superintendent in the 1990s. He commended my determination and commitment. I had worked on an enquiry resulting in five offenders responsible for kidnapping, blackmail, assault, and robbery receiving lengthy custodial sentences. Alas, my Chief Superintendent received a two-year prison sentence for fraudulently stealing £26,000 in expenses, which slightly tainted my award.

Another award was in 2005. My Chief Superintendent commended me for my excellent detective skills, hard work and dedication. My certificate read, "Following a Crown Court trial, the judge sentenced six men to a combined total of one hundred and eighty years in prison for murder." My commendation was somewhat tarnished by my Chief Superintendent committing suicide the day before his two-million-pound fraud trial was due to commence.

Commendations were printed on 'B' Division orders and displayed around police stations. They acknowledged the commended and encouraged others to follow suit. One such award was for an officer who jumped onto a stolen car and held onto the windscreen wipers for dear life. When the stolen car crashed the officer was catapulted into a wall. Though commended for 'Dogged determination and bravery', 'A blatantly obvious attempt to end his own life' was probably more accurate.

In 1981, because the Prosecuting Solicitors urgently required a file I was trying to get into Babs the typist's good books with a box of Milk Tray. My Superintendent walked out of his office, saw me, and said, "I'll take them." He took my box of chocolates and added, "Canteen now, PC Smith." No explanation and without so much as a please or thank you. There were thirty officers and staff already in the canteen. 'Jacko', who worked in admin, was the guest of honour and had completed 'thirty years' service. Jacko was fifty years old; he was a husk of a human being and looked eighty.

The Superintendent trotted out a few clichéd phrases and handed Jacko a bottle of scotch and my box of Milk Tray. Jacko struggled to hold his presents as his hands were shaking, not from nerves. It looked more like a fairly serious medical condition to me. Maybe it was his lifestyle, the scotch or chocolates that finished him off, but Jacko only lived for a few weeks after retiring. I purchased a smaller box of chocolates, which the typist looked at with contempt. She said she might be able to type my file if she had time. Thanks Jacko.

Fast forward thirty years. Admin had arranged a little ceremony for an officer who had completed his thirty years. After a twenty-minute wait, the phone rang, it was the retiring policeman he apologised profusely. His reason for being late? He had run his third marathon that week, which had taken him slightly longer than anticipated. How times had changed.

It was time for my appraisal with my Chief Inspector, Joan Francis. I had been well written up by my shift supervision, probably because they had used up all their poison on Phil Arnold. It was all going well until my Chief Inspector proposed calling the police driving school about the possibility of my attending a driving course. She needed me in a panda car, patrolling her patch as soon as possible. I was flattered but explained I did not have a driving licence. Her smile disappeared. "Officer, stand up, put your helmet on and follow me."

She stood up and put on her police hat. I followed her onto the High Street. We crossed the road. She walked into the British School of Motoring, ignoring the customers. She said to a man who looked like he was in charge, "This is PC Smith. He works for me and, quite ridiculously, does not have a driving licence. Please book him ten driving lessons and a driving test as a priority."

The guy opened a diary, made notes, and quoted £80 for ten lessons. I said I would drop a cheque in later. My Chief Inspector told me she did not want to see me again until I passed my driving test. She went back to her office. I did not have £80, and there was no prospect that I would any time soon.

The following day, I went back to BSM and cancelled the lessons. I gave my Chief Inspector a wide berth for a while.

Looking back, Chief Inspector Francis was right. I should have taken lessons and passed my driving test, even if I could not afford a car. I could have attended the police driving school, taken a one-day assessment, and become qualified to drive a police car. Instead, it was another ten years before I became a panda driver.

The officers on the shift continually changed, with only the numbers remaining roughly the same. Sergeant Steve Wagstaffe replaced Sergeant Roberts, who had twitched his way into retirement. Steve joined the shift on promotion from a lengthy attachment to the 'Bomb Squad'. At 4am on nights, Steve asked if I had checked the High Street shops. Even though I said I had, he stood up and said, "Come on, I will show you how to do it properly. Follow me."

Steve led me out of the station. When we came to the first shop, Steve took a firm hold of the door handles, vigorously rattling them to confirm they were secure. He said, "That's how you do it, Wolfie. Old fashioned coppering."

We continued, and Steve firmly rattled more door handles. After precisely fifteen minutes, the alarm on the first shop activated. The alarm bells' deafening sound split the night. Shop alarms had a fifteen-minute delay. The other shops' alarms joined in at one-minute intervals, creating a cacophony of noise.

A flustered controller was rounding up the troops to deal with what appeared to be the looting of Kings Heath's shops on a previously unseen scale. A sheepish Sergeant Wagstaffe radioed in, "Sergeant Wagstaffe to control, cancel the troops attending the High Street. I know what the problem is. I will pop back and explain. I will leave Wolfie here, and he can deal with the keyholders as they arrive." While Steve had been on his attachment, shops had fitted sophisticated intruder alarms.

I became mates with D Unit's Mark Blackburn and a Moseley beat officer, Hughie McGowan. Neither was interested in learning to play 'Go', so we enjoyed a pint or two whenever possible.

Working on B Unit was like the cliché about policing, 'no two days were the same.' I cannot remember many fallouts. We were too busy to allow personal issues to get in the way of police work. My role varied between front office duties, an observer in the zulu or footpatrol.

Even working in one of the front offices had its moments. At 5.30am, I took over from PC Ron Tiler at Billesley police station. Ron, a bespectacled man with sideburns, had long since decided that police work was not really for him. Ron was counting the minutes until retirement. He rarely spoke and never smiled. Ron had one final challenge left, which he had completed that very morning. Ron looked elated.

Billesley police station had an alarm, and the motion sensor was on the wall next to the clock in the front office. Red - no motion detected, Green - motion detected. Ron sat motionless in his chair for the duration of his eight-hour shift. He focused on the red light and did not even answer the phone. There had been no visitors, and even his sandwiches remained untouched. Ron had completed his tour of duty without moving. Ron shook my hand. He even tooted his horn as he drove off. I never saw him that happy again, but I was glad to have shared his moment. Of course, the Superintendent did not commend him for his achievement, but the certificate could have read,

"Through pure dedication and commitment, PC Ron Tiler worked an eight-hour shift at Billesley police station and never fucking moved once."

I am unsure if it was just luck, but I was in the right place at the right time and received further commendations. My new Chief Inspector, Roger H Bagley, had noticed my arrests. In April 1981, while walking past Mr Bagley's office, he saw me pointed and indicated that I should join him. The lovely Joan Francis had moved on, so I no longer feared being dragged across to the British School of Motoring by my ear. He cut short his phone call,

"Morning Wolfie, nice arrest the other day," I resisted the urge to say, 'Which one?'

"Thank you, sir."

"I have a job for you. How would you like to work a beat in Mosely village?"

How would I like to work a beat in Moseley and leave the physically demanding and draining shift pattern? Like it? I would love it. I kept it short.

"Sir, I would relish the challenge. When can I start?"

Mr Bagley explained he needed to resolve one issue. I offered to leave to let him deal with whatever the problem was. He told me to sit down, picked up his phone, dialled a number, and said, "Is that Woodbridge Road? Good, Chief Inspector Bagley here. To whom am I speaking? Excellent. PC McGowan, your time on the beat has come to an end. You are being replaced and will start on C Unit from Monday. Find out their shift pattern, and do not be late."

That was good news for me, but not for my mate Hughie. With only fifteen months in the job, I had my own beat to police, Moseley Village.

CHAPTER 7

MOSELEY VILLAGE - THE PROMISED LAND

The day I started at Woodbridge Road, Moseley, so did Yvonne Morgan, and I was delighted. We joined on the same day and, after Ryton, worked on different shifts at Kings Heath. Yvonne is black bubbly and grew up in Birmingham. She was intelligent, funny and had an explosive laugh. The beat officers already at Woodbridge Road were Chris Taylor and Kevin Mills. Our sergeant, Nick Fisher, was public school-educated and a devout Christian. Years later, he became a Reverend Doctor in Oxfordshire, but in 1981, his staff and Moseley's population were his flock.

The beat officers shared an office at the rear of the station, which didn't have a door. The CID office had a door that was rarely left open. Val, the typist and Sergeant Fisher shared the middle office. Val was so good at her job that all she needed to produce a Crown Court file was an officer's pocketbook. Val extracted and typed all the necessary statements and the case summary. She added a witness and exhibit list. It all looked extremely professional. Val also pointed out any evidential or continuity errors. I worked with many typists in my service, but Val was the most talented.

Kevin Mills borrowed a panda car. I needed an item from the detained property store at Kings Heath, so I joined him. Kevin was a big bloke and only happy when assisting at the local scrapyard. Compared with the rest of our team, he was taciturn, and a grunt from Kevin was the equivalent of a full-blown chat with anybody else. Kevin pulled into the yard at Kings Heath. Mick Mears, driving a CID car, was blocking our path. Mick had six months less service than me. Looking back, I could have selected a more sympathetic ear to whinge into other than Kevin's. "How has <u>he</u> got onto the CID, Kev? I've got more service than him."

Kevin was annoyed but only by the delay preventing his return to the scrapyard. He never even turned his head,

"I can think of two reasons. Firstly Mick can drive a car, and secondly, he is not a cunt." Silence reigned for the rest of the trip. I was sulking, and Kevin returned to his factory default settings.

Yvonne and I partnered up to patrol Moseley Village. While we were in Alcester Road, the controller asked if anyone could attend a burglary in Park Hill. We were not far away, so we went. Yvonne rang the doorbell, and an elderly lady, probably in her late seventies, opened the door. Yvonne sympathetically said, "I am so sorry to hear your house was broken into overnight, my dear. It must have been quite a shock."
The old lady stared through Yvonne. We awkwardly waited on her doorstep. Yvonne said,

"I don't suppose you know who broke into your house, do you?"

The lady glared at Yvonne. I was beginning to feel uncomfortable. Finally, the old woman spat out, "Who burgled my house? I'll tell you who I think it was. Probably your brother, love."
I felt like I had been punched in the stomach. Somehow, Yvonne muddled her way through and obtained the necessary details from the racist crone to complete a crime report.

I recently spoke to Yvonne about the incident. While she didn't dispute it happened, she couldn't remember it. Conversely, I never forgot it.

Kevin was spending more and more time at the scrapyard. It was no surprise when the CID executed a search warrant at the premises and recovered dozens of Police National Computer printouts for vehicles, all obtained unlawfully by Kevin. They contained useful information for the scrapyard owner - registration details, engine, and chassis numbers. As well as stolen and police interest reports. The West Midlands Police sacked PC Mills a few weeks later.

In only a few months, I witnessed the dismissal of a probationer and a serving police officer. I'd also seen how quickly a beat officer could find themselves back on a shift.

I decided to get my head down, work hard, and attract my Superintendent's attention to my triumphs rather than disasters.

A week is said to be a long time in politics. Five days in July was all it took to turn policing in the West Midlands on its head.

On Sunday, 4 July 1981, the Handsworth Carnival took place. A Times newspaper reporter described the event, "I found eight thousand black and white people in a spirit as amiable and peaceful as any rural village fete. It was an excellent example of successful community policing."

Five days later, following a West Midlands Police Superintendent's inept speech to calm the community's fears about a proposed National Front march, the area turned into a battlefield. The disturbances resulted in one hundred and twenty arrests, forty injuries to police officers and millions of pounds worth of damage. There had been rioting in other areas of the country, including Brixton and Moss Side. But in Toxteth, the disorder was so violent that the police used CS gas on the English public for the first time.

On Sunday, 11 July, the West Midlands police assembled all available officers to patrol the streets of Handsworth. After our parade, we used single-decker public transport buses that the police had appropriated for transport. We had no protective equipment, and one officer had not even brought his truncheon.

Waiting at a holding area, the door to the bus opened, and a sergeant threw a carton the size of a large box of crisps to our Inspector. Everyone on the bus stared at the box, a moment later recaptured by the film *Seven, 'What's in the box?'*

The Inspector opened the box and pulled out wafer-thin visors. It wasn't much, but it was all we had. He demonstrated how to secure the visor to the helmet - using only an elastic band and a slit that fitted onto the peak of the helmet. Once fitted, it flapped about, and I doubt it would offer protection from a sneeze. I needed one. It was apparent there

was not enough to go around. Remember my whiny voice when I bleated to Kevin Mills about Mick Mears? Well, it resurfaced, hopefully for the last time. "Sir, I need a visor."
From the back of the bus, someone shouted,
 "Oi sprog, there's a queue, and you are at the fucking back of it."
 "You don't understand. I need a visor. It's because... I wear contact lenses."
Pathetic though I sounded, an officer threw me his visor, but the elastic broke when I tried to fit it to my helmet.
 A review of the public disorder suggested several factors that had contributed - distrust of the police, racial tension, inner-city deprivation and copying events elsewhere. When the situation had calmed down, I returned to my beat in Moseley until the next time.

 Margaret Thatcher announced that July 29 would be a public holiday. Her decision allowed the British public to enjoy the TV coverage of Prince Charles and Lady Diana's wedding. It captivated the nation. I watched and tried to find the moment when Camilla took a drag on her fag and whispered to Diana, "You do know I emptied Charles this morning, darling." Sadly, I never found it.
 I started to get around my beat, speaking to residents, teachers, shopkeepers and licensees. I introduced myself to the homeless and the prostitutes. I explained that they had to move on after I spoke to them. If they didn't, I would radio for another officer to attend and then deal with them at the police station.

They understood the rules, so I never had a problem with the parish's drunks or prostitutes. Another group of people I was keen to strike up a relationship with and recruit were informants. They came in all shapes and sizes with various motives - revenge, reward, dislike, but sometimes, they just wanted to do the right thing. It was my job to sift out the crackpots among them.

A few weeks after the riots, the Birmingham Evening Mail published a two-page spread of CCTV captures showing offenders looting shops in Birmingham. One photograph captured an Asian man exiting Curry's through a smashed window while holding a camera with the price tag still on it. His smile looked like he had posed for the picture. I recognised the smile, but even though I didn't know his name, I knew I had seen him somewhere in Moseley.

I wasn't sure what to do, so I photocopied the picture onto A4-sized paper with the header, 'Wanted by PC Wolfie Smith, Woodbridge Road'. I used Sellotape and stuck posters on the lampposts in Moseley. I waited. The detectives at Woodbridge Road ridiculed my efforts, "The dozy sod thinks he's Wyatt Earp, working at the OK Corral."

A month later, on a hot summer afternoon, I was on footpatrol in Church Road. A man wearing an overcoat and a balaclava sidled up to me. He must have been bloody warm. He lifted his balaclava and said, "Yo Wolfie, I believe you are looking for me."

He was an Asian man who looked a bit like the man on my wanted poster, but when he smiled -

BINGO. I acted cool and listened. His name was Tariq Zaeem. He showed me his driving licence and asked, "Wolfie, can you arrest me on Monday? I am on my way to a job interview, and it will look much better for me at court if I've got a job."
I thought for a moment and decided, fair enough. After all, Zaeem could have walked past me. I shook his hand, and we agreed on 1pm. My actions were an 'Acting on my own initiative while showing determination and commitment' type of commendation. That was what I thought, anyway.

I knocked on the CID office door, and Detective Sergeant Bruce called me in. After briefing him, Bruce said I should have nicked Zaeem straightaway, and if he came in on Monday, I should speak to one of his detectives for guidance. Then, as I left his office, he told me that once I obtained a confession I should take all the embarrassing wanted posters down, smartish.

On Monday at 1pm, as good as his word, Mr Zaeem turned up at the front counter at Woodbridge Road. I arrested and cautioned him, then took him into the PBO office. I popped into the CID office and briefed the only detective there. I showed him the photograph and told him the circumstances. He said I should take a defendant's statement and get a "Full and Frank admission" - Detectives liked using that expression. Then, charge the prisoner with burglary and take three sets of fingerprints. The additional set was a breakers card - for burglars.

In his interview, Zaeem explained that he had been in Birmingham when everybody went crazy. Somebody smashed Curry's window, and everyone grabbed stuff and ran off. The camera he stole wouldn't work as he didn't have the instructions, so he chucked it away. I charged him, and he shook my hand and apologised. I left all the papers on the detective's desk as instructed.

Zaeem received a six-month prison sentence following a guilty plea at the magistrate's court. I heard nothing, no Queens Police Medal or invitation for a glass of champagne with the Chief Constable.

A month later, I saw Inspector Colin Young at Kings Heath police station. He called me into his office, closed the door, and asked how I was settling in at Woodbridge Road. I told him I was enjoying myself. "Can I give you some advice, Wolfie?" I nodded, so he continued, "One of the detectives at Woodbridge Road is a bit special, and you need to hang onto his coattails and learn as much from him as possible." He told me how the detective arrested one of the looters from Birmingham, and all he had was a photograph from the Evening Mail.

Hmm, this sounded gut-wrenchingly familiar. Mr Young continued, "He posted the newspaper photograph all around Moseley. Then, using his network of tried and tested informants, he tracked the offender down, arrested and charged him. The looter received a custodial sentence, good old-fashioned police work, Wolfie, as I said, you could learn a lot from him."

"That's amazing, sir," while thinking, 'The sneaky bastard'. I had done the heavy lifting while the detective took all the credit. I was not the only probationer who got turned over by a detective. In many ways, it was a rite of passage.

From that day on, I heeded the advice of Elvis Costello -*Watching the Detectives.* Not to learn from them but to work out the ones I could trust. I needed somebody who understood and could explain how this police malarky worked.

On cue, Steve Hollowood arrived as a beat officer at Woodbridge Road. Steve was good-looking, intelligent, and confident around police work and the female of the species. Steve had seven years more service than me, most of which he had spent as a detective.

Steve joined the beat officers at Woodbridge Road following a fallout with his Detective Inspector. His DI showed Steve the report that put him back in uniform and asked what he thought. A far-from-flustered Steve responded. "Well, given the space provided and your pathetic command of the English language. I think you have done an excellent job." Steve Hollowood would teach me a lot.

At 8am on Tuesday, the lollipop lady from the Infant and Junior school in Oxford Road reported sick. That crossing patrol was a priority, and the controller told me to cover it. Steve wasn't doing much and accompanied me.

At the school, I walked into the centre of the road, stopped the traffic and started crossing the parents and children. Steve stood by a lamppost and smoked a crafty fag, which he cupped in his hand. I tried a bit of banter with the children, "Come on, kiddywinks. Remember, these are the best days of your lives." One disillusioned seven-year-old grumbled, "Well, that doesn't give me much to look forward to then."

Steve had seen enough. He finished his cigarette, expertly flicked the butt down a drain, walked into the road, and took over. An attractive Mum held her five-year-old son's hand, waiting for Steve to stop the traffic. As they crossed the road, Steve spoke to the lad, "Come on, son, let's get you into school. I bet your big sister needs to get to school when she has dropped you off." Steve winked at me. The now-blushing Mum fluttered her eyelids and said,

"Thank you, officer. I actually have three children, and Jimmy here is my youngest."

"You are joking," said Steve, feigning shock. Then, having dropped Jimmy at school, Mum crossed the road again, paused when she got to Steve and whispered into his ear.

When the crossing patrol finished, Steve quietly said, "Wolfie, you might think an infant school is just about little kids, but it also means yummie mummies." Steve added, "I'll tell you something else." His voice dropped to a whisper. This appeared to be top secret, possibly the nuclear launch codes. "Most women who have kids at school don't want any more children, so they are on the 'Jack and Jill', you know, the pill." Was there anything that Steve didn't know?

I returned to Woodbridge Road on my own. Steve had to attend an address in School Road to do with something that had only recently come up, apparently.

When he returned to the nick, I nosily asked, "How did you get on at School Road?"
Steve put his cigarette out, "Wolfie, I would have already told you if I wanted you to know. If I don't

want you to know, I will tell you lies. So it's probably best that you don't ask."

I had an abundance of enthusiasm but no experience. Steve advised me to run to a fire and walk to a fight, explaining performing heroics at a burning building could result in medals, awards and newspaper headlines. In contrast, arriving at a fight too quickly could earn me a punch in the mouth. When in a house, Steve told me to block the entrance to the kitchen, as it is full of knives and other weapons of mass destruction.

I arrested a man on suspicion of the theft of a wallet. I did not have a lot of evidence, only a witness who had seen someone who 'looked a bit like' my suspect hanging around the area. It wasn't much, but it was a start.

In the PBO office, my prisoner went on the attack, "Look mate, you're wasting your time. You've got no evidence, so just let me go." I explained that I only needed to ask a few questions about where he was at the time of the theft. Steve arrived for work and was hanging up his jacket in our office. Steve had no idea who I had arrested or why, but he could tell things were not going well, so he just took over, "Alright, son, wind your neck in and allow me to explain something." The prisoner and I were all ears. Steve continued, "Wolfie will ask you a few questions, but it is all down to you. I will write the file the judge will read at court and paint one of two pictures. A young man who has made a silly mistake and apologised for his actions. Or a little shit who needs to be sent to prison as he is a fucking menace to society. It makes no difference to me. It's your choice." The prisoner asked for a minute or two to think.

Steve and I left him to stew, "Wolfie, I didn't mean to take over like that, but I thought you needed a bit of help. You do know I will not be doing your file, though."

"No problem Steve, I appreciate it. I assume you will have to be getting off now."

"What makes you say that?"

"I don't think you have dowsed yourself in Paco Rabanne aftershave for my benefit. I will catch you later." A sweet-smelling Steve smiled and left the station.

My prisoner admitted he had climbed into his neighbour's garden and stolen a wallet from a jacket. He handed me the wallet and received a police caution for theft.

A couple of days later, while on footpatrol with Steve, a man on the other side of the road was someone I wanted to speak to. I left Steve, nipped across the street, and after a short conversation, rejoined Steve, who asked, "Who was he?"

"Steve, if I wanted you to know, I would have already told you. If I don't, I will tell you lies, mate." Steve chuckled and said, "You're learning, Wolfie."

When we returned to the nick, I dug out a crime report and made some notes. Steve asked if my writing had anything to do with the guy I had just spoken to. I confirmed it was, and he had given me the name of a suspect for a theft.

"A word to the not-so-wise Wolfie. Never write a suspect's name on a crime report. Most detectives could not detect a fart in an aqualung and go through your basket when you are not in, desperately looking for clues. Writing suspects' names on crime reports is one of the reasons detectives refer to their uniform colleagues as *woodentops*." He made one last point,

"Never reveal the name of an informant. Tell even one person their details, and everyone in the nick will know who they are within a day. Even the bloody cleaner will ask if your grass is still coming across." Thank you, Steve - more words of wisdom for his young apprentice.

While Steve was tutoring me, he also assisted Yvonne and Chris Taylor. We would all help each other, but Steve had the experience we lacked.

I policed football matches at all the top midlands clubs - Aston Villa, West Bromwich Albion and Wolverhampton Wanderers. *What about Birmingham City?* I said the top Midlands clubs.

Steve and I were part of a large contingent of police officers policing a packed Villa Park. Aston Villa, incredibly, won League Division 1 (Now the Premier League) that season. We patrolled the pitch perimeter and ensured that fans stayed behind the fences.

Suddenly, a red-faced Superintendent jogged down the terraces and ran towards us. I could add that to the list of things I had never seen before and was unlikely to see again. I thought, this must be important.

"Oi, you pair of pansies, what are you doing? You're practically bloody holding hands. Are you two getting married anytime soon?" Wow, a Superintendent who could see into the future and accepted the concept of single-sex marriages thirty-three years before they became legal in this country.

I cheekily explained, "Sir, here's the thing - we have to be together. Steve here can't throw a punch, and I can't take one."

The Superintendent told Steve to trot on. And warned me that if I got within thirty yards of my colleague, I would spend the rest of my tour of duty in the police detention room.

Moseley Rugby Club was on my patch, and I watched Mark Linnett play and develop while playing for their first team.

I occasionally policed the County cricket games at Warwickshire, but I was always required for the sell-out Test matches at Edgbaston. Being paid to watch some of the finest cricketers on the planet was a real perk of the job.

I learnt the basics in training and the routine and discipline on the shift, but Steve covered subjects not taught in any classroom. We were at the scene of a criminal damage. An elderly lady's neighbours' children had damaged her fence, and she reported the matter to the police. The victim was a crotchety old woman who gripped her walking stick with a degree of menace. If I asked her age, I feared she might chop me in half, but a victim's date of birth was required on all crime reports. Steve must have read my mind, "Right then, my dear, let's get the kettle on, but before I make you a nice cup of tea, I need to ask how young you are?"

"You cheeky monkey. I'm eighty-three."

"Sorry, did you say fifty-three?" The flattered old lady smiled and said to me, "Oh, I do like your friend."

Even violent prisoners were not a problem. A prisoner left for us to deal with was in the cells at Kings Heath. According to the custody record, it had taken six police officers and a lengthy struggle to get the man into a cell. He had booted his cell door throughout the night and issued threats to all and sundry. He was only arrested for criminal damage, but I was concerned for my safety. Steve said, "Come on, Wolfie, watch and learn."

Steve took the key to the cell and opened the door. The Incredible Hulk stirred. As cheery as you like, Steve said to him, "Come on son, let's get you a cup of tea, get you interviewed and take you home." We obtained an admission and a full and frank apology.

Steve explained to me it is a part of everyone's DNA that anyone liberated from a place where they are being detained looks upon their rescuer as a friend. I used that approach for the rest of my service.

I joined Kings Heath Squash Club, which was on the 50 Bus route. Squash was a good workout and only took forty minutes. I represented the club and played in league matches and tournaments. Steve said he fancied taking the game up and 'went off to buy a bat'. I think his enthusiasm only got as far as purchasing a racquet.

Steve used squash as an alibi to be elsewhere. While my smelly kit waited to be taken home and washed, Steve rinsed his gear under a tap, so it looked like he had played.

At 8pm on a Saturday, Steve and I were on footpatrol in Moseley Village. Steve noticed several cars parked on the pavement outside a curry house. The restaurant attracted wealthy patrons who owned expensive cars. Keeping their vehicles in view while they enjoyed their meal probably made sense.

Steve walked into the restaurant, and I followed. Steve kept his helmet on and asked to see the owner. Then Steve pointed out several cars parked on the pavement. Following a conversation that ebbed and flowed, they reached an impasse. Steve said, "Fair enough if that's how you want to play it. Wolfie, get your fixed penalty pad out, and let's get these vehicles ticketed." An interesting bluff by Steve, as neither of us carried fixed penalty pads.

The manager asked if this matter could be resolved without issuing parking tickets. Steve raised his nose and started sniffing. He turned into the *Bisto Kid* and said, "Please, tell me that is not chicken tikka masala I can smell. Do you know that chicken tikka masala, pilau rice, and a garlic nan is my favourite Indian meal?"

Is there a curry house on this planet that does not serve chicken tikka masala? I don't think so. We did not issue any fixed penalty tickets. Instead, the manager accepted the advice about the illegally parked vehicles and said it would not happen again. Steve and I were gracious for the owners' hospitality, though I would have preferred a lamb madras.

Steve and I were on uniform patrol in Moseley. An Asian man stood by the gates to his drive, which led to his large detached house. He called us over and asked if we could assist. "I have loads of bloody foxes in my back garden, causing absolute havoc. They are up all night fucking and fighting. Is there anything you can do?" None of this sounded like a job for the police. I stood back and waited for Steve to give the man the bad news.

Steve whipped his pocketbook out and took down the man's details. Then asked, "Okay, Mr Khan, how many foxes are causing the problem?"

"Seven or eight, officer."

Mr Khan and I were tuned in.

"Right then, Sir, I think I can resolve this." Steve put his pocketbook away. "I will speak to the master of the Moseley Hunt as soon as we get back to the station."

"The Moseley Hunt, what the bloody hell is that?" asked the concerned resident.

"It's all legal, forty riders on horseback, aided by thirty hounds that will track and kill the foxes. The foxes that survive will shit themselves and never come back. This will soon be sorted, my friend."

"Whoa, horses and dogs running around my fucking garden. I am not sure about this."   Steve reassured him, "Don't worry, someone on the hunt will blow a horn, so you will know they are coming. Stay inside until they are gone. Shall we say next Thursday?" Mr Khan looked terrified.

"Actually, officer. I will just contact the Council. But thank you anyway. Please do not send the Mosely Hunt unless I get back to you."

As we walked away, Steve was behind me. I looked back and saw Steve pissing himself laughing.

I enjoyed my time with Steve. It might have been boring for him, but I never forgot his advice. He was one of a kind. Steve moved back onto the CID. I occasionally saw him socially, but there was no point in asking him where he was working or what he was doing only to be told, "Wolfie, if I wanted you to know, I would have told you… etc."

Hughie joined me for a pint in the Bulls Head and had been to Tally Ho the night before. Hughie said he had seen Steve Hollowood in full gigolo mode. Chit-chatting, smiling, fluttering his eyelids, he even threw in a little Spanish to impress the policewoman he was chatting up. After listening to Steve schmooze for ten minutes, Hughie said he felt aroused. After twenty minutes, Hughie said he would happily have let Steve take <u>him</u> to bed.

When I wrote Full Disclosure, Steve bought a copy. He asked if he was in the book and sounded disappointed when I told him he wasn't. On reflection, I realised that he definitely should have been.

A word about the silver-tongued lotharios in the police - they appeared to have a wonderful life, flitting from female to female. However, appearances can be deceptive. They worked hard to receive sexual favours, having to continually shower gifts and compliments on their paramours. It was not all fluffy pillows and sex.
One married officer confessed to being involved with two other women. Though the sex was worth the

effort, one Christmas day, he had to eat three dinners lovingly cooked by the women in his life. He said he was more stuffed than any of the turkeys he had eaten.

Though it was an expression used to describe other officers, sadly - "Vince Smith only uses police vehicles to ferry his genitals from one female to the next" - has never been said. In my defence, I was not qualified to drive police vehicles until my mid-thirties.

Another mate, rather popular with the ladies, got dragged to the cinema four times to see 'Titanic' - a movie named after a boat and the film's length. At the time, it was <u>the</u> film every woman had to see with the man they intended to share their life with. For years, even the mention of the movie caused him to twitch.

On 31 January 1982, I was on duty at the Reddings for the Rugby Union County Championship final between Lancashire and the North Midlands. The great Bill Beaumont captained Lancashire. He was also the England captain who led his country to a Five Nations Grand Slam in 1980.

The County final was a hard-fought battle. Beaumont suffered a concussion in the second half and had to be assisted off the pitch. He never played competitive rugby again. It was the end of an era. Beaumont's consolation was that Lancashire won a low-scoring match, 7-3. Mine, well, I could always say I was there.

CHAPTER 8

DAD IN JAIL AND A DEATH IN THE FAMILY

In 1982, the Birmingham pop band Dexys Midnight Runners had a number-one hit with *Come on Eileen.* The cook at single mens quarters at Woodbridge Road was called Eileen. There is absolutely no connection between the last two sentences.

Dad had a key to my house and popped in to help himself to a cup of tea whenever he was passing. There was a good reason why I did not have a key to my dad's flat.

In 1978, when I worked for Redditch Council, my Dad lived five minutes away from the Council offices. I sometimes ate a bag of chips in his flat, while I read one of his never getting returned because they didn't know he had it, stolen library books.

One lunchtime, I popped into his flat. There were dozens of Polaroid photographs scattered around his lounge. I picked up a couple and quickly wished I hadn't. They captured my forty-eight-year-old father entwined with a lady half his age, and they appeared to be working their way through the *Kama Sutra*. Dad's flat door opened, and he waltzed in.

"For God's sake, Dad, couldn't you have put these in a drawer?"

Rather than embarrassed, he looked pretty proud and said,

"You have to see this picture, son."

Incredibly, he started to hunt through the snaps, trying to find his favourite. I didn't know what to say, so I fished the key to his flat out of my pocket and handed it to him,

"Dad, I won't be coming back anytime soon, you dirty old sod."

A documentary about the Thames Valley police hit the news headlines. A lady attended Reading police station to report that she had been gang raped. Initially, the victim was dealt with by two caring uniformed officers. Then, three experienced male detectives took over, and that was when Roger Graef's documentary became television folklore.

Viewers were outraged by the detectives' badgering the victim throughout her interview. One detective assessed the victim's account as "The biggest load of bollocks I have ever heard in my life." Surely, he had to know something the rest of the watching public did not. Well, as it turned out, he didn't.

The nation was incensed, forcing the Thames Valley police to launch into action. For his five minutes of 'keeping it real and telling it exactly how it is,' the 'load of bollocks' detective was rewarded with an immediate return to uniform duties. The Thames Valley police appointed five sexual-offence trained policewomen to handle their rape enquiries for the foreseeable future.

Over breakfast in the police canteen, a discussion about the programme took place. One of the crusty old detectives chipped in, "Typical, the public doesn't want to know what happens in the real world. I don't know why we bother." Most around the table had never dealt with a rape victim or suspect, so we stayed quiet. Mick, another detective, asked Crusty, "Hey, do you remember the test we used on victims alleging that they had been gang-raped?"

Something sparked in Crusty, and he remembered, "Oh yes, she was given an old wooden chair to sit on, with no cushion or padding. If she was comfortable sitting on that chair, she definitely hadn't been fucking gang raped. It worked every time." The detectives chortled while the rest reflected on what had been said. Throughout the country, police forces showed Roger Graef's documentary as an example of how <u>not</u> to treat a rape victim.

I was getting around the residents on my beat and gaining their confidence. Some offered information about the local ne'er do wells. Receiving intelligence felt like being a press reporter with a scoop. But it had to be acted upon before anybody else heard the same information. My informants kept the prisoner entries in the back of my pocketbook, ticking over.

DC Colin Abbotts, a top detective on the CID at Woodbridge Road, selected me for an undercover operation. It was a one-man mission scheduled to take place the following day. Colin sat down with a cup of tea and briefed me. He had bought a house in Solihull and was in the process of buying new furniture. Lush Furniture on Kings Heath High Street was an upmarket store, and Colin had selected the three-piece suite he wanted for his lounge. It was identical to the one on display. He offered to accept the display model provided a sizeable discount was allowed. The salesman insisted that Lush Furniture - *La De Dah* - did not do that sort of thing.

With the suite scheduled for delivery on Monday, Colin was concerned he would receive the on-display suite, albeit cleaned and covered in polythene. I was to attend the shop and mark the underneath of the master chair with the green felt tip pen he handed me. He also supplied a hand-drawn map indicating where the suite was in the store. Colin threatened that my future progress in the organisation could depend on the outcome of this mission.

On Saturday morning, walking into Lush Furniture, I looked more like someone in the market for a pint of cider than a customer buying quality furniture. A keen salesman, who I think just wanted me out of the shop, asked if he could help. Without a cover story, I said I was browsing - pathetic. When the salesman spotted an actual customer, I seized my opportunity, but damn, I couldn't get the felt-tip pen under the chair to make a mark.

Determined to complete my assignment, I reached underneath the chair. The salesman looked at me but was probably satisfied I could not shoplift an armchair. I pulled out a large staple and pierced my right index finger. I drew blood, marked an 'X' with my finger, and felt woozy. The salesman, who had tolerated my presence long enough, curtly suggested that Kings Heath's public library encouraged their visitors to browse. I phoned Colin and explained why the cross underneath the chair was red, not green.

On Monday, the manager of Lush Furniture made the delivery. Colin told him to bring the master chair into his lounge. He unceremoniously removed the plastic covering and turned the chair upside down. Colin angrily explained why a red cross was on the bottom of the chair. An extremely embarrassed store manager apologised and offered Colin a massive discount for the suite. Colin paused, and the manager improved the offer, which Colin accepted.

On Monday, Colin saw me, "Wolfie, any more blood and the chair could have been classified as a crime scene."

Woodbridge Road single men's quarters housed eight policemen. They were mostly on shifts, so their comings and goings were not a problem. The main issue was when they enjoyed consensual recreational sex. Their cries of passion could be heard in Moseley village.

DC Ned Kelly was interviewing a suspect in the CID office. He started jabbing the ceiling with a broom handle while shouting, "For fucks sake, I am trying to interview some joker down here for an armed robbery. So keep the noise down, you animals." The copulating couple took a break, shut their window, then resumed, unperturbed.

Britain declared war following the Argentinian invasion of the Falkland Islands on 1 April. Many people thought the Falklands were near Scotland's north coast. In fact, they were almost 8,000 miles away in the South Atlantic.

In April, my sister Kathleen, who lived in London, was rushed to Balham Hospital. She was suffering from anorexia nervosa. Shortly after her admission,

Kathleen consumed a tray of the other patient's prescription drugs and collapsed into a coma.

I visited her, and though she looked like the beautiful young girl I will never forget, the prognosis was not good. The doctor said a ventilator was the only thing keeping her alive. Kathleen was only twenty-three years old.

I sobbed my heart out on the train journey home. I phoned the hospital for updates, but the only change was the mood of the nurse who took my call. If she was happy, my sister was "Much perkier this morning." Otherwise, it was a gloomy, "I am sorry, but there has been no change."

For years, my Dad ignored all correspondence about Frances's child maintenance, and the courts finally ran out of patience. I received a letter from HMP, Winson Green, Birmingham, which, as it turned out, was my dad's new address.

As he was no longer Anthony's sole guardian, the magistrates took the opportunity to send my Dad to prison for twenty-one days, which both penalised and wiped his slate clean. Frances was twenty-one at the time.

The fact that Kathleen was on a ventilator and fighting for her life would never have been a good enough reason for Mum to waive her maintenance arrears. My brother described our Dad's punishment as "Like rubbing a dog's nose in a shit it had done years ago."

While my Dad was a tobacco baron in 'C' Wing, Britain was still at war in the South Atlantic.

Aston Villa had fought their way to the European Cup Final, and on 29 May, Villa beat the mighty Bayern Munich 1-0. Courtesy of a ball bouncing off Peter Withe's shin and into the back of the net. The Villa brought home the European Cup for the first and probably the only time in their history.

Prime Minister Margaret Thatcher was having a torrid time and desperately needed something to galvanise her position. On 20 June, she re-captured the Falkland Islands at the cost of nine hundred and seven lives.

The following day, I received a phone call from one of my mother's sisters, Sadie. She told me Kathleen had died in hospital and would be buried in Hereford Cemetery the following day at 2pm. Mum had tried to get the service conducted before the news broke. Yes, she could be that spiteful. It was also possible Aunt Sadie thought my side of the family's attendance could spice up proceedings.

I caught the train to Hereford with my wife, son, brother, and father and attended the service. We all went home after the burial. That was the last time I saw my mother. On the night of our sister's funeral, my brother can tell you Russia drew 2-2 with Scotland at the World Cup in Spain in front of 45,000 spectators.

CI Bagley selected me to work with John McAnneny, one of the beat officers who had tutored me when I joined. We worked in plain clothes, and our mission was to target an outbreak of burglaries in the Moseley area - the posh part.

We had a bit of luck on our second day. At midday, we rushed to the scene of a house alarm in Amesbury Road. A caller said they had seen two men running from the house seconds before its alarm activated.

On arrival, a sweating man rushed across the road and seemed keen to get away. He didn't notice the twigs and leaves in his hair, but we did.

I stopped the man and asked for his details, and he gave me a false name.

Top tip - if you have dozens of prison tattoos, don't give the police a name that does not exist on the Police National Computer.

The man eventually gave his real name, Brian Warren. He had escaped from HMP Nottingham and had six more years to serve for a series of burglaries. Johnny Mac arrested Warren.

DCI Bond, who was in charge of the CID, decided that Warren should be returned to Nottingham prison to complete his sentence and not charged with any further offences.

DC Colin Abbotts, whose court files were exceptional, joined Johnny Mac and me on the burglary team. Force intelligence linked Warren with Nathan Davis to burglaries all over the West Midlands. West Mercia Police also wanted Davis, as he had left his driving licence at the scene of a burglary in Studley. Davis's family lived in Redditch, and our infrequent forays to find him were unsuccessful.

The Redditch Detective Sergeant dealing with their investigation was Dave Willetts. Dave teased us that he was odds on to capture the elusive Mr Davis before we did. Interestingly, Davis's midlands criminal record number was 8293, which is my collar number. Maybe it was a sign.

One Sunday, Dave Willetts phoned Johnny Mac and told him Davis was in custody at Redditch. Davis was available to us, but as he had not said a word since his arrest, we would probably be wasting our time seeing him.

John collected me en route to Redditch. He was smiling and said he knew something Dave Willets didn't. We declined Dave's kind offer of a coffee and asked to see Davis. Dave introduced us to the custody sergeant and said once Davis had told us to 'fuck off,' he would come down for a coffee and a chat.

After two minutes, Davis asked if we could take him to Kings Heath police station so he could admit a series of burglaries that he had committed with Warren. Dave Willetts was perplexed. We bid him a fond farewell and offered to assist if he had any other serious crimes he was struggling with.

John pointed out to Mr Davis that his last four appearances at Crown Court were at Worcester. On each occasion, he received a five-year prison sentence. The only way Davis could guarantee an appearance at Birmingham Crown Court was to admit offences committed in the West Midlands. Ensuring he would not meet a pissed-off judge who had sentenced him on a previous occasion. Davis knew enough about the system to realise this was definitely to his advantage.

Davis admitted six burglaries, all committed with Warren. Colin Abbott's experience kicked in. Colin's actions resulted in both suspects appearing at Crown Court charged with several burglaries.

Further statements were required. Colin and I called to see one of the victims, who lived in a large detached house in Edgbaston. He was a senior English lecturer at Birmingham University. Colin jotted down a brief statement containing the details a court required for a burglary complaint. He handed it over to be signed; the lecturer looked at the statement and then took out his red pen. After a few minutes, the lecturer handed back the unsigned document. Spelling mistakes, grammar and punctuation errors were all highlighted and circled. I saw Colin was about to explode, so I suppressed my giggles. An angry Colin said, "Right, I can see from your ridiculous scribbles you have read your statement. So can you now take my pen and sign here and here." For clarity, Colin jabbed his index finger at the signature spaces.

Colin liaised with the Prosecuting Solicitors department and charged both men with six burglaries. At the Crown Court, Warren and Davis were sentenced to eight years imprisonment. Warren's sentence was to commence after his current one finished. The DCI threw his teddies out of the pram and commended no one for the investigation.

I popped home one lunchtime, and my Dad was making himself a cup of tea, "Christ, son, you need to sort out your life. I've just had a shit, and you don't have any frigging toilet paper in the house."

"Okay, Dad, I will get it sorted."

"I had a mooch about, and I've had to use a snotty tissue that I found in the little bin beside your bed."

My heart skipped a beat. That wasn't snot. It was a bodily fluid, but not from my nose. If anything happened to my Dad and he died, a post-mortem would find traces of my semen on his bum. In my mind, I pictured myself standing before the Coroner, "Well, PC Smith, before I call the Forensic Scientist to confirm the detailed findings from your father's post-mortem. Please explain to this court the details of your sexual relationship with your father?"

My Dad finished his tea and said he would be getting off. I hugged him and told him to be careful. That was not how we usually parted. Dad gave me a strange look as he left.

I didn't hear from him for a month, so when he phoned, I actually punched the air in relief

In September, the Chief Constable formally appointed me as a Police Constable. I could still get sacked, but it required a little more effort from the organisation.

I was either working my beat, on a squad or on a shift if their numbers were depleted. I might never have been wounded on duty if not for my time back on C Unit. I was with John 'Greetings' Moore, a Zulu driver loaded with charisma and panache. We arrested a feisty young man for criminal damage, and John decided the prisoner needed handcuffing. I was grappling with the lad's hands. John applied the handcuffs with a little more force than usual. The three of us heard the sound of skin ripping. It only took a second. Then, I realised the inside of my right thumb had been sliced and separated from the bone.

John had caught my hand in the handcuff ratchet, and my blood spurted everywhere. I was in pain. John was concerned, and the prisoner was silently amused. The scar remains visible to this day. I never pressed charges.

My colleagues encouraged me to buy a house. I found a semi-detached property in Arundel Crescent, Olton, near Solihull, that I was interested in. It was priced at £25,000, a fortune at the time. I made an offer, which was accepted. The police contributed a monthly tax-free rent allowance to my mortgage payment.

I needed a solicitor to handle the conveyancing. The lads at Woodbridge Road pointed me in the direction of Martin Jenkins.

I knew 'Jenko' from his days as a Prosecuting Solicitor. He once summoned me to discuss a public order case of mine. I did not have much service, and Jenko felt that my attempt at a case summary fell a little short of acceptable.

"PC Smith, I have read this pile of shit." He held my file away from him like it was a dog turd and continued, "You don't need a solicitor, it's a fucking magician you require. I've read between the lines and worked out that the defendant has had a slap. So this case is going nowhere." He continued, "However, I have spoken to the defendant's brief, and he will accept a bind over."

After our inauspicious start, we got on well. Martin had recently started his own practice and was looking for business, and we struck a deal. I was buying a leasehold house and instructed Jenko to purchase the freehold.

I moved into my new house on Christmas Eve. Having paid extra for the carpets and curtains, I was extremely disappointed to discover the owners had wallpapered around the wardrobes and cupboards, which they had taken. Their carpets were fitted around the furniture they had taken as well.

I could search the planet for matching wallpaper, carpets, cupboards and wardrobes or resign myself to redecorating and carpeting the house. The cooker, which the vendors had kindly left free of charge, did not work and hadn't for some time. It cost me £10 to have someone take it away. Thanks a lot. I enjoyed my cheese and tomato sandwich on Christmas day. I suppose I could have phoned a lothario and offered to take his place or accompany him on one of his many Christmas dinner invites.

Work was now two bus rides away, but the area and schools were much better. As for the neighbours, we got on fine.

My marriage was, unfortunately, on borrowed time. Enjoying as many nights out with Mark and Hughie as I could afford probably didn't help. I think you either became closer or drifted apart, and we were sailing away from each other at a rate of knots.

CHAPTER 9

GONE FISHING

Moseley had so many layers; it was fascinating. I was on first-name terms with the homeless, alcoholics, prostitutes, some of Moseley Rugby Club's first team and Pete the Feet. It was a small and friendly community. Dave Cox, the butcher, charged police officers only 25p for a breakfast bag containing - an egg, bacon, sausage and a bit of black pudding, all ready to be fried up, back at Woodbridge Road.

Socialising on my patch sometimes caused a problem. Early one evening, Sergeant Joe Mullen was controlling and called me on the radio. "Can you attend the Trafalgar pub? Reports have come in that Jimmy Doyle has gone absolutely ape-shit in the bar. Update me as soon as you can. I will get hold of more officers, but only if you need them."

Joe was a Geordie and always said it like it was. However, I now had a problem. A few weeks before, there had been a kerfuffle in the Trafalgar. I had done nothing wrong, but that was not how Bob Sayce, the licensee, saw it.

"Sarge, is there anyone else you can send?"

"Wolfie, there is no one else available. Are you too scared to go?'

"Sarge, I can attend and give you an update, but I have had a violence on licensed premises form served on me. So legally, I can't physically go into the pub." I could hear Joe chuckling down the radio before he said, "Sort it out, you numpty."

I walked to the pub. Bob Sayce was outside, saw me and said quite loudly, "Not you, Wolfie. You are still barred." How embarrassing. I waited outside until Jimmy Doyle had finished wrecking the place and arrested him as he walked out.

At Woodbridge Road, beat officers left and were replaced. The newcomers were delighted to have escaped the shift pattern. The ones who left were looking for even greener pastures. I liked the area, the people and even some of the criminals. I knew it wouldn't last forever, but I lived in hope. Anyway, my bus pass did not pave my way onto any specialist departments.

My marriage ended in March, and my wife returned to Germany to live with her family. Peter stayed with me, and we coped as best we could. As a treat, I took him to Birmingham to see his first-ever film at a cinema, *ET The Extra-Terrestrial*. I was worried it might be a bit much for him, as he was only two. He lapped it up, and a lifelong love of movies possibly started there.

When we left the cinema, I popped into a bookshop and bought him a picture book about the film. It was one of those shops where you signed up to join their book club. While that book only cost £1, I spent three years trying to leave the book club. Every month, I received their book of the month. Which, according to the robbing bastards who ran the book club, I had agreed to accept.

In June 1983, Margaret Thatcher won her second general election. She crushed the Labour Leader

Michael Foot, a brilliant politician famed for his House of Commons speeches but who the British public thought was useless. Besides, Maggie Thatcher had won the Battle for the Falklands, and the British public loved any leader who had won a war.

I liked Maggie, as she gave me a pay rise and stopped the free school milk, which meant children did not have to go through the ordeal I had faced at school - milk blended with teachers' cigarette smoke. Mrs Thatcher was preparing for another battle she would fight much closer to home.

On Friday, 18 November, Nick Fisher enquired whether I had any plans for the weekend. Consulting my social diary, I confirmed that I had no plans for either that or any other weekend in the foreseeable future. Nick invited me to join him and his friends at Twickenham for England's match against the New Zealand All Blacks. I asked how much it would cost, and Nick said we would sort something out. He advised me the dress code for the day was a jacket, shirt, and tie and to be at Woodbridge Road at 9am sharp. While I was excited to attend a top international rugby match, not knowing the cost terrified me.

I caught the coach with thirty of Nick's social circle. In case we became separated, Nick handed me my ticket for the match, which was for the East Upper Stand and priced at £9. (I still have the ticket stub.)

My word, Nick's friends were posh. So I dialled down the swearing in my vocabulary and mentally rehearsed, 'Gosh - what a blinking good tackle, Dusty'.

On route to Twickers for the 2.30pm kick-off, we stopped at a Country Mansion for lunch. Rounds of drinks, none of which I bought, were served. Nick ordered me a roast beef sandwich, a must-have, apparently. I only had £10 cash, which only just covered the cost of the ticket and an emergency cheque, which was tucked behind my warrant card. Financially, I was sweating.

The match was a gruelling physical encounter. Luckily for England, Dusty Hare had brought his tackling and kicking boots. He slotted over four penalty kicks, and England won 15 - 9. Someone from our party produced a hip flask and offered it around for a celebratory tot whenever England scored.

On the way back, we stopped for a meal. I enjoyed the peppered mackerel starter, Beef Wellington main course, and an Eton mess, followed by cheese and biscuits. All washed down with a bottle of Chateauneuf-du-Pape. After the meal, the wine continued to flow like…wine, I suppose. I was now officially squiffy.

At midnight, our coach pulled into Woodbridge Road. I quietly asked Nick Fisher how much I owed for the day and braced myself. "Don't be silly, Vince, the chap who dropped out quite happily paid for your match ticket and refreshments. Perhaps I should have told you earlier." I was both grateful and relieved.

Working a beat required things to be done in a certain way to make the job easier. So if I needed to speak to someone, a witness, suspect or victim, then at a reasonable time, I called at their address. Though

I only spoke to one person, the entire street tuned in. The police visiting anywhere was always a reason for curtains to twitch. Announcing and reinforcing what a reasonable chap I am, I left my contact details and returned a few days later. If that failed, I returned at an unreasonable hour, and they only had themselves to blame.

Serving summonses on defendants was the responsibility of the beat officer who covered the area where they lived. I swiftly learned that no one admitted to being the person named on a summons. I developed my own method of deception, which helped. I would attend an address, knock on the door, and ask the occupant,

"Are you Mark Davies?" - Or any other name <u>not</u> on the summons. The relieved guy who answered the door confirmed that he wasn't.

"No problem. Can I ask what your name is?"

"Michael Noonan."

"Oh, hang on a second, sorry, this summons is for Michael Noonan." Served the papers, and that was the job done.

No-Bail warrants were easy. If the offender failed to surrender during the week, I left their arrest until after 12.30pm on a Saturday. Once detained, the next available court hearing was 10am on Monday, and they spent two nights in the Central lock-up. My beat area was so small I could visit most addresses during my tour of duty, so my message was clear. I was not going away.

In December 1983, The Flying Pickets, an acapella pop group, had a number-one hit with *Only You*. It would not be long before the 'Flying Pickets' would be in the news again, and it would have nothing to do with the music charts.

Some of the incidents in Moseley were a bit different. I was on patrol in Moseley when the controller, Geordie Joe, shouted up on the radio, "Wolfie, can you and Bill Bailey attend 71 Reddings Road? I cannot make head nor tail of what has occurred, but the two old bats who live there have called the police and are properly upset. Good luck."

With all the sobbing, it took a while, but we established the old ladies' two cats, Minky and Muffin, had been missing for a few days. I listened, sympathised and even made them a cup of tea in their silver teapot, which I poured into their posh china cups. I updated the controller. He shared his thoughts, "Right, this is not a matter for the police. You and Bill carry on with your footpatrol. Anyway, with the number of curry houses in your area, they have more chance of finding Minky and Muffin if they order a chicken Balti from Imran's."

My brother was doing well at school. He played football for his school and was enjoying proper meals and electricity. In June, he took his GCEs. (A year later, they were replaced by GCSEs.) They seemed to have gone well, and he had no intention of returning to school. Instead, he started work at a factory in Kings Heath.

When the posh people from Moseley met, the working-class oiks, sparks or even hammers could fly. A Residents Association Chairman was standing on the pavement when a vehicle performing a three-point turn reversed onto the pavement and almost hit him. The chairman decided to 'have a word.' Following the incident, his witness statement read,

"A car reversed slowly onto the footpath and was only inches away from me. I was infuriated, so I knocked on the driver's window, rat-tat-a-tat-tat... tat-tat. The car driver, a fat man who was smoking, wound his window down. He looked pretty angry, so I used sarcasm to make my point. 'Excuse me, I think you will find this light grey bit, where I am, is actually the pavement, and the dark grey bit adjacent is called a road, which is where your car should be.' The driver muttered something and lodged his cigarette in his mouth. He reached behind into what I now think was a toolbox, selected a hammer, struck me in the face and broke my nose." Another offence filed under - this did not need to have happened.

For some obscure reason, I decided to join ten other Kings Heath policemen on a sea fishing trip. I have always said, 'Give a man a fish, and he can eat for a day. Teach a man to fish, and he will bore the arse off you for the rest of your life.'

The plan was an early Saturday morning journey to Swansea, eight hours fishing on a boat in the Irish sea, then a night on the beer. Mark Blackburn was the only real fisherman. The rest of us got our fish from the freezer section at Tesco. I went along for the *après-fishing* piss-up and a night on the town.

Mick Butler, who recently joined the job and had a degree in Zoology, advised us to eat Digestive biscuits as it had been clinically proven they prevent seasickness. You cannot argue with someone with a degree that ends with 'ology'. I had not even thought about being sick. I had caught the ferry to Ireland many times and never had a problem. Like the rest of the group, I bought a packet of digestives.

I stood beside Bill Bailey on the boat and cast my line. We were chatting, and I gave it a few minutes. I slid my left hand across my body and nudged the butt of Bill's fishing pole. When his float bobbed, thinking he had caught the first fish of the trip, he ripped his line out of the water with such force Mark Blackburn said, "Bloody hell Bill, if your hook had attached itself to the boat, you could have turned it over."

Brian Bridgewater chipped in with, "Whatever it was, Bill… I think you've ripped its lips off."

That was when the fun stopped. Ten minutes into the trip, while our little boat floated on a sea of digestive biscuit sick, I was gripped by seasickness. I grabbed the metal rail so tightly while retching I am sure my hand indentations are still on it.

I remembered a line from a Spike Milligan book, 'The only cure for seasickness is to sit under a tree.' Unfortunately, neither Spike's advice nor the Digestive biscuits did anything to help. So I abandoned my fishing pole and resigned myself to dry retching until I arrived back on *Terra Firma*.

Someone caught a Conger Eel, a bloody big one. I have mental images of its decapitation and being sliced into steaks, a visual atrocity.

I retched until my stomach muscles were so painful I thought I would die. The Captain of the boat joined me and offered some words of advice. In his soft Welsh accent, he said, "When you get to a little brown chewy bit, boy, don't spit it out, as it'll probably be your arsehole."

Everybody else thought his comment hilarious, but I could not get my hands off the metal railings to take a swing at him.

Eventually, after one of the longest days of my life, we returned to the marina. I decided I was never, ever, ever going to get on a boat again.

We all had a quick shower and changed out of our smelly clothes at the family-run Bed and Breakfast we had booked. Then, we set off to visit the fleshpots of Swansea. I was recovering from my ordeal on the boat. It was the only time I was out with Brian Bridgewater when we did not have a Guinness drinking competition.

At about 9pm, two Welsh ladies in their forties who had scrubbed up for a night out sort of attached themselves. While walking towards another pub, one of the ladies said they needed to say goodnight to their husbands but were keen to stay with us for the remainder of our pub crawl. Was this how women in Wales behaved? One of the women cupped her hands around her mouth and screamed, "Goodnight, Frank."

A male voice replied, "Goodnight, Brenda."

The other woman screeched, "Goodnight, Darren."

A male replied, "Goodnight, Pauline."

The large, drab building the women were shouting at was Swansea Prison. I don't know if Darren and Frank would have sounded so happy if they had known their wives were gallivanting around town with a gang of coppers.

Having had quite enough of shifts, Mark Blackburn became a beat officer at Woodbridge Road. Mark selected a desk and started work. The first problem Mark identified and addressed was <u>me</u>. Mark always looked smart, whereas I went for the more weather-beaten look. Mark declared I looked like a bag of shite. He grabbed a bin bag, dug out as much uniform as possible from my locker and drove me to Bournville Lane clothing stores.

Percy was behind the counter, and not many got a word, let alone an item of equipment from him. Percy firmly believed the stores were for storing uniform, not handing it to police officers who treated it as disposable. Percy's standard response when asked for an item of kit, "I'm sorry, officer, that is as difficult to get hold of as rocking horse shit."

Mark slapped the bin bag and contents on the counter and instructed me to remove my tunic and trousers. Percy could see Mark meant business, so he attempted to stall proceedings,

"What if I haven't got anything in his size ?"

"Well, that would mean Wolfie will patrol Moseley in his vest and underpants tonight. Superintendent Walters may phone you and ask for an explanation, Percy."

Percy tutted, grabbed the pile of rags on the counter and disappeared out the back

Fifteen minutes later, with a pinched face and eyes narrowed, Percy returned with an armful of uniform, which he put on the counter. He looked like a man handing over the family jewels at gunpoint. I put on a new pair of trousers and a tunic, they nearly fit. What a result.

When we returned to Woodbridge Road, Mark handed me his boot polish, so I gave my Doc Martens a much-needed clean. I brushed my uniform, sorted out a fixed penalty pad, and updated my pocketbook. We walked out of Woodbridge Road and were ready for anything. We made the mistake of turning left. Bob Sayce, who had only recently lifted my ban, was outside the Trafalgar Inn, "Evening, officers, my goodness, you're looking extremely dapper this evening. Would you care for a pint of your usual?" Able to resist anything but temptation, we walked into the pub. Mark muttered under his breath,

"I don't know why I even fucking bother…"

In March 1984, after some political posturing, Maggie Thatcher and Arthur Scargill stopped sparring and were 'Ready to Rumble.' The Mining industry went on strike. When an 'Iron Lady' instigates a battle against a man with one of the worst comb-overs in history, I suppose there can only be one winner.

The Government deployed police officers nationally to deal with the public order problems caused by the conflict. 'Flying Pickets' travelled the country in vans, assisting the miners who needed support. The police attempted to keep the peace, whether it was a massive gathering like the battle at Orgreave or collieries with local issues between 'scabs' and strikers.

Proteus Army training camp in Nottingham was my first miners posting in June 1984. We had a van, a sergeant and ten officers. Unfortunately, the Metropolitan Police had been in Nottingham the week before. The Met driving around and waving £20 notes at the miners shattered the police and miners' already fractious relationship.

Police officers paid off debts and upgraded their holidays. The dispute lasted almost twelve months. I never saw any real action, only long hours, poor food and terrible accommodation. On the plus side, financially, it was extremely rewarding.

When several high-profile criminal cases collapsed during Crown Court trials, the media slaughtered the judicial system, and the police also took a lot of flak. So, in 1984, the Police and Criminal Evidence Act came into effect.

The changes in the law meant tighter guidelines and more accountability. The police had a lot to learn. The training department could not update every officer, so they issued a green PACE book containing the new rules. To avoid ridicule and humiliation at the hands of the solicitors who attended to defend their clients, I gave that book my full attention.

CHAPTER 10

THE BULLS HEAD, BORIS AND BOB GELDOF

In Moseley, The Bulls Head was my watering hole of choice. It was full of characters. The banter was both brutal and hilarious. Pete the Feet would take on all comers at Backgammon. Pete went on a winning streak, but because he played against Hughie and me, a couple of dodgy patrons suspected Pete was a police informant. They believed the cash we handed over was how we paid him to be our 'snout'. Hughie McGowan added to the quality banter and had his darts ready to accept financial challenges on the outcome of a game of arrows.

The barman, 'Concorde', had a nose so bulbous that it actually honked when anyone punched it. Robin Pryke dressed and looked like 'Dr Who,' complete with a long scarf and a glamorous lady assistant, Rea, from Canada. As far as I could ascertain, his income came from a professional gambling collective that delivered him to racecourses and plonked him next to the finish line. The syndicate waited for his verdict on the photo finishes, then bet heavily on Robin's selection.

Johnny Giro was a hard-working manual labourer who was equally committed to receiving full state benefits, so he was always double busy.

Dave Yates was a 'flyman'. I didn't know what that meant and had to ask. He worked at The Alex Theatre in Birmingham. With a harness attached to the stage wires, Dave took to the skies and hey presto - 'Peter Pan'.

Though Bob Monkhouse hogged the limelight on ITV's 'The Golden Shot', a lesser-known icon from the same show was 'Bernie the Bolt'. I knew him as John Baker, who popped into the Bull's Head for a pint and a giggle during the week. Then, on a Sunday night, he loaded the all-important bolt onto the crossbow. Before the whole, "Up a bit, down a bit, right a bit. Fire" decided whether the contestant went home with the star prize or a cameraman dived for cover.

Steve Ajao was almost seven-foot-tall, a saxophonist and singer known as a blues/jazz performer in Birmingham's music circles. So it was hard to refuse when he asked, in his deep, syrupy voice, for only £5 for his latest CD recording.

Gordon was a dour Scotsman and not a big fan of Hughie or me. One night, he was digging away at the both of us, "You're a fucking pair of wasters. For fucks sake, anyone in the West Midlands Police with half a brain usually makes it to Chief Constable. But look at you two, 'PC Do-little and his faithful sidekick PC Do-even-fucking-less." Gordon was about to cross the line from caustic banter and step into the, probably getting thumped by Hughie zone.

Jim, an elderly gentleman in his seventies who <u>was</u> a fan of me and Hughie, stepped in,

"Calm down, Gordon. What is your claim to fame, that you can give these two such a hard time?"

"Jim, for one thing, I made my first million when I was only twenty-two."

"Gordon, that is amazing, absolutely astonishing, and I didn't know that. I have to say that I would give you an incredible amount of respect for that achievement. If I fucking believed a word of it." Gordon finished his single malt and left.

Damien, a tall, thin man with a ginger perm, managed Corals, the bookmakers opposite the pub. Damien would share gambling tips and whispers. Colin Egan, a cockney, was ex-army and a good bloke. With the jesting talents of Micky Flannagan, he was the glue that held the group together. The Bulls Head rarely had proper fights, though the occasional battered ego required a period of recovery.

It is always difficult to compare eras, and I greatly admire the work of JRR Tolkien. It is only my opinion, but I think the Bulls Head in the mid-eighties had more characters than the 'Prancing Pony'.

A skinhead called Richmond Wayne Wilson lived in Moseley. He was a small man who spent his time sniffing glue or thieving. As he was pathetically feeble, he made sure his robbery victims were frail or old. Despite his non-descript build and fairly common Birmingham accent, Wilson's single distinguishing feature made his identification reasonably straightforward. Underneath his left eye, he had the word 'SKINS' tattooed.

A crime report arrived, and I skimmed through the victim's statement. It read, "All I can remember about my attacker was that the little shit had 'SKINS' tattooed under his left eye."

Within half an hour, Wilson was cornered and arrested in St. Mary's Church cemetery by

Woodbridge Road's dynamic duo, Chris Taylor and Mark Blackburn. They escorted Wayne to the Kings Heath custody suite, where the delightful Sergeant Felix O'Neill awaited.

The rotund Felix wore a police shirt, and the last time its top button had been fastened was when it was in its packaging. His police tie was clipped onto the breast pocket of his shirt. Felix, as always, was smoking and drinking a can of Coke - not diet. Felix was approaching retirement and had long since lost all faith in humanity. Which was reflected by the wording of his questions to prisoners on their arrival,

"What do you say your name is?"

"What do you say your date of birth is?"

"Where do you say you live?"

Wayne was charged and remanded in custody.

Pleading guilty to the robbery at Crown Court, Wilson received a three-year prison sentence. Full of remorse and licking his wounds, Wayne declared he was going straight, getting a job and letting his hair grow. However, if he continued to offend and kept his tattoo, he would never be hard to track down.

On footpatrol in Moseley Village, Chris Taylor and Mark Blackburn were walking behind two hippies. One was chanting,

"Boomshanka, Boomshanka hashish for sale." The other turned and said,

"Oi, back off, fascists. You are invading our personal space, man."

Mark responded, "If you call me a fascist once more, sonny, I will stick my jackboot so far up your arse, it will tickle your tonsils." You can't beat a bit of friendly banter with the locals.

Boomshanka - though it sounded offensive, it meant - May the seed of your loin be fruitful in the belly of your woman – Neil from The Young Ones 1982.

Mark and I were on patrol when a man ran out of a derelict house in Balsall Heath. He sprinted off when he saw us, and Mark ran after him. I set off in pursuit of Mark. The man was getting away, so Mark started throwing things at him. Helmet, truncheon, police radio, a bin lid and even his tie? Eventually, by following the trail of uniform, which I gathered, I joined Mark and the man he had detained.

Mark had recovered an axe from the man's waistband as well as some cannabis from his jeans. Mark said I should have been with him, right on his shoulder. Mark was a rugby player, and that's how they talked. In my defence, I said I had been busy collecting his kit. After our last visit, Percy would never have replaced it - Mark sort of agreed.

We took Mark's prisoner to Kings Heath's custody suite. We lodged him in a cell, the axe in the detained property and the cannabis in the station safe. The controller instructed us to attend Birmingham Crown Court immediately. The courts pre-warned civilian witnesses, whereas police officers were often summoned with only a few minute's notice.

At 5pm, after hearing our evidence, the Judge dismissed the case, so we went off to drown our sorrows

The following day, Mark and I started work at 10am. Felix, now the controller, told us to get to the DI's office at Kings Heath pronto. Felix also suggested we put telephone directories down the back of our trousers as we were about to get our arses tanned.

During one of our late-night drinking sessions, Mark asked if I had a contingency plan for when I dropped deep in the shit. I didn't. He did, "Wolfie if I get called in to see a senior officer, and he has me bang to rights. I will stand up and start screaming while ripping the fly buttons of my trousers. Then run out of his office, shouting, 'He has just grabbed my cock'. Let's see how he fucking explains that."

The DI remained seated in his office, though he wasn't much taller when he stood up. He explained that all drugs seized after 3pm should be lodged in the drug safe at Bournville Lane, and failure to comply was a disciplinary offence. The system had changed, and neither Mark nor I were aware. I had been in the Army for nearly six years and was used to being bollocked. Mark had not served in the Army.

The DI started issuing threats, which washed over me. He was going to put us on a charge. We would never be allowed onto the CID. So far, so good, but then he upped the ante.

"What I should do, though, is give you both a good hard kick up the arse." It never bothered me but infuriated Mark, who responded, "Sir, with all due respect - *and then proceeded to show him no respect whatsoever*- you can discipline us. You can stop us from getting onto the CID, but you are not fucking big enough to kick our arses. Vince, come on, let's get back to Moseley." Purely out of loyalty, I followed Mark. The fly buttons on Mark's police trousers remained intact, no doubt to be ripped off on another occasion. I was three or four hours away from my personal bollocking threshold.

On 13 April 1985, I was on duty at Villa Park for an FA Cup semi-final between Everton and Luton. Both sets of fans shared the Holte End and were separated by a line of police officers. I was one of those officers. Policing an FA Cup semi-final was a real perk of the job. Kevin Sheedy was playing for Everton that day.

I was at Secondary school with Kevin and in the same class as his older brother, Michael. Michael's Mum transported a team to six-a-side football competitions held at fetes in country villages during the summer school holidays. I was lucky enough to be part of the team. We were the 'Tram Inn', named after the Sheedy's pub, and we usually won the tournaments. Despite his age, Kevin was always one of the best payers on the pitch. Michael had a superb left-foot shot, but Kevin had a magic wand for a left foot.

The Sheedy family went on an African Safari holiday one year. Michael gave me a small hand-carved elephant with ivory tusks as a souvenir of his trip. The last time I saw it was when Mum launched it at my Dad's head during one of their many violent domestic disputes.

At sixteen, Kevin signed as a professional footballer for Hereford United. He transferred to Liverpool before signing for Howard Kendall at

Everton, where he settled and became a legend. He played for the Republic of Ireland in the 1990 World Cup and scored their equalising goal against England.

Returning to the FA Cup semi-final, Luton were by far the better team and deservedly took an early lead. With time running out, Everton won a free kick on the edge of the Luton penalty area. Kevin Sheedy tucked it away with aplomb, and the match went into extra time. With only five minutes left, Kevin Sheedy, with absolute precision, delivered a free kick onto the head of Derek Mountfield, which he powered into the net. It was a great game, and my schoolboy chum had played his part in Everton reaching the FA Cup final.

The miner's strike ended in March 1985. With the same determination that she had reclaimed the Falklands, Maggie Thatcher crushed the mining community.

A distressed lady from Allenscroft Road, Waldrons Moor, Kings Heath, called the police. Her husband was en route to the hospital, and she urgently needed to speak to a police officer. I attended, and the controller asked for an early update.

The distraught lady explained that her creepy neighbour had popped around with a homemade steak and kidney pie. Despite her concerns, her husband tucked in. Before he had finished, he started vomiting. She called an ambulance, which took her husband to the hospital.

I borrowed a bin bag and seized the remnants of the pie and the sick covered tablecloth. The police radio didn't work in that area, so I used the lady's telephone and updated the controller, who briefed the CID and confirmed they would turn out to assist me.

I answered a knock on the front door. It was the creepy neighbour he asked to speak to me in private. I informed the lady I would only be away for a few minutes.

In the man's flat, I saw a cookbook on the kitchen table, it was opened at the steak and kidney pie recipe page, which was interesting. Even more significant was a bottle marked 'poison' next to the cookbook.

I arrested the man for administering poison with intent to cause grievous bodily harm. I cautioned him, then seized the cookbook and poison as evidence. Though I told the suspect to be quiet, he couldn't help himself, "He is a brute of a man and needs to be taught a bloody lesson." I wrote down his comment in my pocketbook.

Eventually, a detective sergeant arrived and took charge of the investigation. He relieved me of my prisoner, the evidence, and the leading role in the crime papers. During the poisoner's formal interview, he tried to minimise the offence.

"I tested the poison on myself, you know. I was not trying to kill anyone."

As an unemployed council bin man, he could not convince the Crown Court that he had the necessary scientific skills to administer a dose of poison that wasn't potentially lethal. His defence was kicked into touch by the judge, and he was sentenced to four years imprisonment.

I started a six-month attachment to the Kings Heath CID. I thought I was in the right place at the wrong time. It might have been different if Johnny Mac had been there, but he was on the CID at Bournville Lane.

I couldn't drive, which meant I was unable to run errands. Plus, I had no intention of fingerprinting every detective's prisoner just because they couldn't be bothered.

Things were not going well, and after a couple of weeks, the DI reduced my six-month attachment to three months. I did not do myself any favours either. My not-very-tall Detective Inspector received dozens of letters from a company that sold inserts for shoes that promised to 'make you look taller.' The DI had no evidence, but he knew I was responsible. The department could not wait for me to leave, and I could not wait to go. I pottered around and dealt with prisoners.

Sergeant John Mason from my B Unit days was on the CID. He was investigating a series of robberies and had identified a pattern. The offenders used vehicles purchased from Measham Car Auctions, which was only open for business on a Wednesday afternoon. The offenders used the car to commit a robbery on a Thursday and then abandoned and burnt out the vehicle. The cars they purchased only needed to remain on the road for a day, so they fell into the cheap and not very cheerful category.

On a Wednesday at midday, DS Mason and I set off to the Measham Car Auctions. As an afterthought and in case our mission was successful, we popped into the local police station in Ashby-de-la-Zouch. Sergeant Mason needed to know how long their officers would take to attend and assist if it kicked off at the auctions.

We walked through the station door, which doubled as a time portal into the 18th century. Sat behind the desk was the oldest police constable I had ever seen. Grey hair, grey beard and a uniform generously sprinkled with dandruff. He was puffing away on a pipe of *Basil the Great Mouse Detective* proportions.

The office man growled, "What do you two want?" Sergeant Mason responded.

"We are from the CID in Kings Heath in Birmin…" He was rudely interrupted.

"I asked what do you want? Not, can you tell me your fucking life story."

John Mason explained to England's scruffiest, oldest and grumpiest policeman that we were heading to Measham car auctions. Adding that, we may have to arrest several dangerous armed robbers. Sgt Mason had added the word 'armed', hoping to capture the attention of the office man. It didn't. The fossil behind the counter yawned. Then said, "Well, best of luck with that. Though I don't see what any of this has got to do with me."

John Mason was seething, tried to remain professional, and then didn't.

"Do you think we have called into your station so that you could wish us good luck? You useless senile twat."

"Well, just out of interest, why have you come here?"

"Well, if it all gets nasty at the car auctions, I need to know how long it will take your fast-response vehicle to come to our assistance, you fucking tosspot?"

The tosspot mulled this over, took a puff on his pipe and said,

"Well, that all depends."

"Depends on fucking what?" Snapped Sgt Mason, who was ready to flip.

"On whether he has been fed or not."

"Who has been fucking fed? Who are you talking about?"

" Our fast response vehicle is the police horse, in the stable out the back."

It was time for us to leave. With as much sarcasm as John Mason could cram into one sentence, he spat out, "Thank you so much for all your help and assistance."

"Honestly, it was no trouble."

We never made any arrests that day, but I will never forget my visit to the police station in Ashby-de-la-Zouch.

After my CID attachment, I returned to my beat in Moseley. One Friday afternoon, the Detective Superintendent at Bournville Lane summoned me. On route, I thought, is it possible the CID wanted to recruit the officer responsible for the arrest of - 'The Steak and Kidney pie poisoner of Allenscroft Road?' Well, as it turned out, they didn't.

At 3pm, I turned up to receive my career assassination. The Superintendent could shaft me, send me on my way, and endorse my personal file in block capitals.

'THIS OFFICER IS NOT CID MATERIAL'.

"Right, PC Smith, I have your three-month report in front of me. It is one of the worst I have ever seen. You will certainly not be transferring to the CID any time soon. So I have to ask, why did you bother to apply for the CID in the first place?"

I paused before I truthfully answered, "I never applied, sir. It just happened."

His response was volcanic, "Do not lie to me, boy. No one gets onto my department without making an application."

"I did, sir."

"Right, you stay right there. I am going to go and get your application. When I do, you will write out an apology. Do you understand?"

"But I never applied." By the time I had added 'sir', he had gone. I waited and waited.

At 4.15pm, I asked the Superintendent's secretary if he was coming back.

"He told me to leave you in his office even if you didn't come out till Monday." He said he was going home and slammed the door on his way out. He looked furious, so you might want to steer clear of him if you know what's best for you."

Geoffrey Dear became the Chief Constable of the West Midlands police and received a baptism of fire.

On 11 May, Birmingham City played their last game of the season against Leeds United. It was Birmingham's largest crowd that year, 24,871. Birmingham had been promoted, so the game's outcome was irrelevant. A full-blown riot broke out.

Tragically, fourteen-year-old Ian Hambridge, a Leeds fan attending his first-ever match, was killed when the rioting fans caused a wall to collapse on top of him. One hundred and forty-five police officers were injured.

Judge Popplewell reviewed the incident and described the carnage as "More like the battle at Agincourt than a football match." The sight of helmetless officers wrestling with hooligans showed the world how poorly equipped West Midlands police officers were.

On the same day, at another football match, Bradford City v Lincoln, fifty-six people died in a fire at Bradford's ground, possibly overshadowing the events at Birmingham. Both tragedies were a precursor for further football-related disasters.

The West Midlands police rolled out a series of public order training days. Officers attended training at the steelworks in Tividale and were exposed to fairly realistic public order scenarios. 'Rioters' threw wooden blocks and petrol bombs at officers wearing the newly issued public order kit and carrying shields in preparation for the riots they could face on the streets of Birmingham.

I told my brother about the training, and I think that was when he decided it was time to move out. Anthony had a vision of standing in our garden, holding a little pop bottle full of petrol. Whilst I ran screaming through him wearing the full public order kit. Anthony moved into a bedsit in Kings Heath within walking distance of his work.

I have always enjoyed tennis and was the Junior Army Singles Champion in 1974. Every year since I was a kid, I have watched the BBC's coverage of

Wimbledon. Damien from the Bulls Head also liked his tennis.

In June 1985, Damien came into the Bulls Head to speak to me. He had been to the Queen's tournament in London. Queens is a grass-court competition played before and often a form guide for Wimbledon. Damien had witnessed a seventeen-year-old German lad, Boris Becker, thrash the established Pat Cash in the semi-final. Damien said Becker would definitely win Queens, which he did, and he was extremely confident he would also win Wimbledon.

Damien bet £50 @ 50/1 on Boris Becker winning Wimbledon. As a bookie, he told me Becker's odds would plummet and to get my bet on as soon as possible, but not at his Corals in Moseley. The historical evidence did not support Boris's chances – he was German, unseeded and seventeen years old. No men's winner had overcome even one of those factors. I bet £20 @ 33/1 that Boris Becker would win.

On 7 July, Boris Becker beat Kevin Curran in the final to win Wimbledon. I had paid the £2 tax on my bet and won £660. Cheers Damien.

With a pocketful of cash, I visited Granada TV Rentals on Kings Heath High Street. I ordered a video recorder, paid a month's rental and purchased ten three-hour VHS tapes.

I collected the video recorder on Friday, 12 July. Just in time for the following day's musical event of the century - 'Live Aid'. A televised 24-hour charity music event organised by Bob Geldof.

I started recording at midday and changed the tapes every three hours. I recorded the entire event for posterity.

On Monday, I checked the tapes to see the quality of my recordings. To my horror, nothing had recorded, not one single minute. I unplugged the video recorder and bagged the videos. Then I set off to return everything and complain to the staff at Granada TV Rentals.

At the store, I plopped the goods on the counter. A lady puffing away on a cigarette asked in a thick Black Country accent, "Alright, Bab, what's your problem?" Her name badge let me know she was called Jane.

I explained my brand-new video recorder had not recorded the Live Aid concert and asked what she was going to do about it. Before she responded, she lit another Benson and Hedges, blew a smoke ring in my direction, and asked, "What do you want me to do, Bab? Speak to Bob Geldof and get all the fuckers back on stage, and do the concert again, just for you."

I hadn't even considered the possibility that Jane from Granada TV Rentals had the connections to contact the seventy-five acts to repeat the gig this weekend. And now I knew she didn't.

Jane handed me a replacement video recorder and suggested I thoroughly check the equipment before recording anything important.

On 24 August, PC Brian Chester, a West Midlands Police firearms officer, shot and killed a five-year-old boy while searching a house in Kings Norton. The deceased was the son of the robbery suspect the police were looking for.

Following a protracted investigation, PC Chester faced a manslaughter charge. After a five-day Crown Court trial, Brian Chester was acquitted and returned to his duties as a police officer.

I was posted to a family open day at The Reddings at the end of August. It was sunny, and families enjoyed the stalls and watched mini rugby.

The guest of honour was Michael Elphick, the star of the BBC series *Private Schultz*. He posed for a press photograph with the lovely WPC Lynn Smith and me. Mr Elphick signed my pocketbook as 'Private Schulz'. After completing his guest of honour duties, he headed for the bar. With his gruff accent and roguish good looks, he was excellent company, told loads of stories, and enjoyed a beer or three.

A few months after the event, I was on a coach travelling to Blackpool. I bought the Sunday People to read on my journey. I flicked through the paper's magazine, and in the showbiz section was the photograph Michael Elphick had posed for at the Moseley fete. Except I had been airbrushed out of the picture. So, for me, it was *Auf Wiedersehen Pet* - Another popular Michael Elphick TV Series.

In September, an arrest in Handsworth caused a violent flashpoint between the police and some locals.

Later the same day, Chris Taylor and I were in a police van with our sergeant at the wheel. As we approached Balsall Heath Park, someone threw a milk bottle at our van. We stopped, and the three of us got out. Near the park entrance stood fifteen or twenty teenagers carrying bricks and bottles. I had no idea what their problem was, but I wasn't concerned, nor was Chris. We played football and cricket regularly with these kids.

Chris and I quickened our pace, as did our sergeant. Chris and I ran to the park while our sergeant ran back to the police van, fired up the engine, leant out the driver's window and shouted, "If it all kicks off, take cover in The Shandar!" Then he drove off.

The Shandar was a popular curry house. Most of the youths ran away, so we spoke to an older lad called Rikki. He said that following the violence in Handsworth, some of the Balsall Heath muppets decided to do a bit of copycatting. He said he'd talk some sense into those he could, but with a genuine concern for our well-being, suggested bringing more officers if we returned.

Sergeant 'Braveheart' returned with an assortment of officers who had come to rescue Chris and me. The owner of the Shandar was hugely disappointed - so many police officers and not a single food order. Our sergeant tried to justify his actions, and for the record, I think he is still trying.

For the next few weeks, I was one of the fifteen hundred West Midlands officers who flooded the Handsworth area to prevent further carnage.

Tragically, between the 9th and 11th September, two brothers were burnt to death in their post office. Two people remain unaccounted for, and thirty-five others were injured. Forty-five shops were looted and burnt out. The cost of the damage ran into hundreds of thousands of pounds. Racial tension and unemployment were considered the major causes of the disorder.

CHAPTER 11

A NEW NICK

Every Superintendent needed to put their stamp on their area, even if it was only changing the car park layout. Beat officers were often used as playdough and moulded into whatever their vision of the future was.

The new Woodbridge Road police station opened on 14 February 1986. Sergeant Malcolm 'Mac' Bradley joined 'Braveheart' as a supervisor. Inspector Dave 'Haggie' Patterson assumed command of Police Fortress Moseley.

Dave Patterson had spent years on the CID. Haggie was the leader of the Internationally acclaimed West Midlands Police Pipe Band. When he walked, he had a bit of a pipe band swirl about him. The grey-haired, well-groomed and unflappable Mac Bradley oozed experience and confidence. Not many senior officers challenged Mac or Haggie professionally. Looking back during their time at Woodbridge Road, I was bulletproof.

I attended the Magistrates Court on a leave day and wore civvies. As I was leaving, a guy asked if he could have a quick word. We turned right into the alley that leads to Steelhouse Lane. "Wolfie, the name's Jim, and I'm only speaking to you because you're not in uniform. Cause where I come from, 'snitches get stitches.' International Stock got robbed last night. I know who did it and where most of the stuff is."

International Stock, Kings Heath, was a large warehouse that sold everything. It was open to the general public. Their stock changed almost daily, so whether you were after a new settee, a table tennis bat or a pair of roller skates, it was always worth popping in for a look.

Jim gave me names, addresses and some details of the stolen property. I asked him why he was doing this, and he said the guys involved were knobs, but he wouldn't mind a few quid for 'grassing' on them. I asked, "Why me?"

"You probably don't remember, but I was in the cells at Kings Heath, and you made me a cup of tea. I asked around, and the word is that you are as sound as a pound."

"Fair enough. One more thing, were you involved with the burglary?"

"Wolfie, I wouldn't do a burglary with those wankers. Oh, and you need to get a move on as the gear is due to be moved tonight."

I phoned the intelligence cell at Kings Heath. The tight-lipped and trustworthy Dave Brown confirmed that burglars had broken into International Stock and stolen goods worth thousands of pounds. He checked the names my informant had given me. One was a frequent flyer, and the others had previous convictions.

I phoned my Inspector and briefed him. He instructed me to apply for three search warrants and return to Woodbridge Road. He said he would round up some troops.

At Woodbridge Road, Inspector Patterson split the officers into three teams. Each took a search warrant and set off to an address in the Kings Heath area. Two hours later, with three prisoners in the cells and an 'Aladdin's Cave' of plunder recovered, the job was a 'goodun'. The three prisoners made full and frank admissions and confirmed no one else was involved.

Burglars, search warrants and recovering stolen property were areas of policing usually dealt with by the CID, and they did not encourage uniformed officers into their domain.

Detectives badgered me throughout the day for the name of my source. If I had weakened, they would have ridiculed my informant and the result. The Detective Inspector's challenge was a little more sinister. He said he knew who my informant was and that he had organised the burglary. Not true.

The suspects were charged and bailed. The stolen property was photographed and returned. I submitted a report asking that my informant, Jim, receive consideration for a cash payment to reward and encourage his continued supply of information.

Two weeks later, a payment of £25 for my informant was authorised. A note at the bottom of the report annoyed me. The Detective Inspector had added, "PC Smith met this informant during his attachment to the CID." That wasn't true.

I told Mr Patterson about my time on the CID and dealings with the Detective Superintendent. I confirmed that I had met the informant the day I applied for the search warrants. He took my report and said, "Leave it with me, Vince."

Mr Patterson drove to Kings Heath and returned within the hour. He smiled, called me into his office and handed me my report. Not only had my

informant's payment been doubled to £50, but the comment added by the Detective Inspector had been tippexed out. I was pleased.
Working for someone who could fight and win my battles was reassuring.

In March, Chief Inspector Bagley summoned me to his office. I was not overly concerned. It was bound to be about the prostitutes or the drunks in Moseley - it always was. Mr Bagley's office door was open, as usual. I think he liked to impress passers-by with his rantings and rollickings. Though he was on his phone, he gestured that I should sit down. I now had a ringside seat to witness the master at work.

Mr Bagley was in a heated conversation with someone. I was not eavesdropping, but from Mr Bagley's eye rolls and headshaking, his call was proving to be far more complicated than he hoped. From what I could gather, this was a request for a uniformed police officer to attend a Catholic funeral mass at St. Dunstan's Church, Kings Heath, on Saturday. Though I could only hear one side of the conversation, it was evident Mr Bagley was tap-dancing blindfold through a minefield, "I am sorry, madam. Two day's notice is not enough time for me to approve your request for a police officer to attend St. Dunstan's." Then, after a long pause at our end, a chastened Mr Bagley replied. "I appreciate you would have also liked to have had some notice before your eighteen-year-old son dropped dead with a brain aneurysm." The lad had intended to join the police when he was old enough, which was her reason for the request. Losing the argument on points, he continued, "Anyway, I don't think we have any Catholic police officers who can attend."

I heard her response because she was so loud, "That's what you think, but you don't bloody well know, do you?"

Mr Bagley was floundering. I mouthed,

"Tell her something has come up, and you will call her back in ten minutes."

The Chief Inspector did just that, and even though he had been on the ropes with the caller, he bounced off them and was ready for a full-blown scrap with me.

"Wolfie, this had better not be some kind of piss-take, or you will be joining McGowan on his shift."

"Sir, as a Catholic, I will happily attend St. Dunstan's church on Saturday."

"Hmm, what shift are you working?"

"Sir, I am on leave, but before you ask, I will not claim overtime."

"Why?"

"I'm only trying to help."

The Chief Inspector picked up the phone and dialled. He told me to stay where I was, as he needed to speak to me. "Hello, Mrs Bulmer. I am so sorry about the interruption, but there was a police emergency that only I could deal with."

He sounded different, almost helpful. Mrs Bulmer must have wondered if it was the same person on the phone.

"Firstly, I don't know what I was thinking earlier. Of course, I will send a police officer to St Dunstan's Church on this occasion. What time is the service? Thank you, and will there be anything else? Okay, in which case, I would like to offer my sincere condolences."

Even though I could hear the dialling tone on his phone. He continued, "I am Chief Inspector Roger H Bagley, the second in command at Kings Heath police station."

With a relieved nod of his head, he put the phone down.

"Right, the deceased's name is John Bulmer, and the service is at 2.30pm, don't be fucking late."

"Is there anything else, sir?"

"Oh yes, I remember now, sort out the bloody prostitutes in Anderton Park Road. I am sick of getting letters from Betty Nosey Bollocks. Carry on."

As I walked out of his office, I said, "You're welcome, sir." But, of course, he had no idea what I was talking about.

The requiem mass was packed and emotional. The family were inconsolable about their loss but grateful for my attendance. John Bulmer's mother thought my Chief Inspector was a knob.

My brother gave me a dodgy cassette with a recording of the comedian - Roy 'Chubby' Brown, 'Britain's most offensive comic'.

Hughie McGowan and I purchased tickets to assess his material for ourselves. We took our seats in a packed Odeon theatre, New Street, Birmingham. In the row behind us sat a family of five - husband, wife and three children, the youngest of which looked about five years old. I was concerned as the material I had heard on the cassette was pure filth and should have carried a government health warning. I thought maybe Chubby's live concerts were less offensive - they weren't.

When 'Chubby' started the second song on his playlist, *I'd use your shit for toothpaste.* I could hear the family behind me get up. As they left their seats, I asked the man why he had brought his kids. "It's her fault, the stupid cow. She fucking booked the tickets." He pointed to his wife, "She thought it was for Dougie Brown. You know, the children's entertainer from the TV." Roy Chubby Brown has been called many things in his long, potty-mouthed career, but never - a Children's Entertainer.

I browsed the housing market and listened to officers who were selling up, cashing in and climbing the property ladder. It was time to move, release some equity, pay off debts, and buy a house a bit closer to a decent school for Peter.

I found a four-bedroom terraced house in Highwood Avenue, Olton that I liked and made a conditional offer. I put my house up for sale and instructed a solicitor to deal with the proceedings.

Within a couple of days, I received an offer for my house, which I accepted. I regularly saw the prospective purchasers of my home as they lived close by. It was all smiles and cups of tea at first. After a couple of weeks, though, their shutters came down, and they started to blank me. I spoke to my solicitor, who fobbed me off, "It's just a legal technicality, Mr Smith, nothing for you to worry about."

I received a phone call from the couple who were buying my house, and their message was somewhat abrupt, "Mr Smith, you do not own the freehold to the house you are selling. We will withdraw our offer if you don't sort this out by Friday. Goodbye."

I made a few calls, none of which calmed me down. Finally, I boarded a train to Birmingham and marched down Corporation Street to Martin Jenkins's office. He looked sheepish but went on the attack, often the best form of defence.

"Wolfie, you wanker, how are you doing? I heard that you got divorced and custody of your kid. You instructed my bloody neighbour Michael T. Purcell. You should have come to me."

"I will come back to Mr Purcell in a minute, Martin, but first, did you buy the freehold for my house in Arundel Crescent like I told you?"

"Does it matter?"

"Well, actually, it does. I am trying to sell my house, and according to the Land Registry, <u>you</u> fucking own the freehold!"
Silence.

"Wolfie, why are you selling your house? It's lovely; I thought you would live there for years." He swallowed hard and said, "Let's go and have a drink, mate."

We went to the pub next door. Martin turned and said, "Wolfie, I will get these in."

"No, Martin, you will get all the drinks in, not just these."

"Fair enough, mate."

Although it wasn't strictly ethical, he said that solicitors often bought property freeholds for themselves. They hoped the house purchasers lived in the house for years. Decades later, when the house was for sale, the passage of time added to life's theatre - divorce, dementia and death, allowed the solicitor to step in and offer the freehold to the new buyers and make a tidy profit. Who knew? Martin agreed to sign over the freehold within two days at no cost. It was the least he could do.

After a few more pints, Martin asked, "Wolfie, why didn't you come to me to deal with your divorce and custody of your lad?"

"Martin, my divorce was fairly straightforward. However, I think if you had any involvement in Peter's custody hearing, there is a reasonable chance he would be living with Eskimos or Aborigines." We shook hands.

An Endowment Mortgage with profits was an affordable mortgage product on the market. The monthly payments were reasonable, only paying the interest every month. The outstanding mortgage was settled when the endowment policy matured.

A retired West Midlands police inspector, Gordon Law, arranged my mortgage. He was the last Birmingham police officer to summon help by using his police whistle.

In January 1966, PC Law disturbed a young man stealing lead from the roof of a school in St Lukes Road, Balsall Heath. PC Law was stabbed by the suspect.

PC Law managed to blow his police whistle then lost consciousness. The swift actions of a nearby resident, who sent his son to investigate saved PC Law's life. The young lad saw a bloodied and unconscious Gordon Law and screamed for help. A 999 call was made, and a police car attended. The officers who arrived did not wait for the ambulance; they drove the critically injured PC Law to hospital which saved his life.

A nineteen-year-old man was charged with attempted murder and sentenced to ten years imprisonment. In 1967, police whistles were replaced with personal radios.

With no further issues, we moved into our new house. The carpets I had paid for were in place, so I assessed my neighbours as law-abiding citizens.

One Sunday afternoon, I was on my bed reading. My front garden was tiny, and Highwood Road was adjacent. My bedroom was at the front of the house, and Peter was on the bed doing some colouring. An ice cream van pulled up outside and played an annoyingly loud jingle. Peter enjoyed ice cream as much as most kids, and I waited for him to ask for one, nothing. The ice cream van repeated its jingle, but again, nothing. I put my hands behind Pete's ears and clicked my thumb and middle finger as loudly as possible, but there was still no reaction from Peter. I was concerned.

My doctor confirmed that a glue build-up was blocking Peter's ears, and he required surgery. She reassured me that this was reasonably common in children. I left the doctors holding a referral letter for a consultant, Mr Shenoi. I phoned him, and he said there was a two-year NHS waiting list for patients to be treated.

I had medical insurance with the police, but I had no idea how it worked. So, in a complete flap, I phoned the Police Federation. The lady who answered told me to stop shouting and calm down. She authorised my son's appointment with Mr Shenoi as a private patient.

A month later, Mr Shenoi operated on Peter at the Parkway Hospital in Solihull. He restored Peter's hearing by draining his ears and implanting grommets and t-tubes. Mr Shenoi monitored Peter's condition and performed further operations over the years. Apart from the occasional ear infection and not swimming, Peter was fine. Mr Shenoi always referred to Peter as "A super little chap."

CHAPTER 12

RUMBLINGS AND RUMOURS

In May 1987, I arranged a lunchtime drink for my fellow beat officers at Billy Millers' pub - The Warstock. I hadn't broadcast the event because those who needed to know about it did. Disappointingly, Chief Inspector Roger H Bagley found out and captured me as I walked past his office. "Oi, knob jockey, get in here and take a seat."

"And what can I do for you, sir?" I asked as I sat down.

"It's about your planned afternoon of debauchery at the Warstock pub. I note that you do not have a bar extension for the event. So, let me make it crystal clear to you and your cronies. If there is no extension, I will turn up at 2.30pm, shut the pub and watch you lot cry in the car park until it reopens at 5.30pm."

"No problem, I'll get it sorted."

"You'd better," said Roger H.

I popped into the licensing officer's office. I explained I needed an afternoon bar extension and hadn't applied for one before. He was a bit busy, so he gave me a blank form and handed me a folder of previous applications to find one I could copy. It took about ten minutes. I gave Mr Bagley a thumbs-up as I walked past his office.

After my successful application, Chief Inspector Bagley ambushed me as I walked past his office. "Get in here, tosspot, and don't bother sitting down."

"What's the problem, sir?"

He was seething, "Well, the magistrates have approved your licensing application for a function titled." He read it from my form, "The Kings Heath Beat Officers Annual Summer Ball."

"Sir, I copied the title from…"

"Shut up; firstly, May is not in the fucking summer, is it? Secondly, Billy Millers' pub is a spit-and-sawdust shithole, not Kensington Palace. I also doubt that champagne cocktails will be served on arrival or that carriages will arrive and collect guests at 10.30pm. And I assume the entertainment will be you and Blackburn performing hand-to-hand combat with some of the locals." I started to speak, and he put up his hand to stop me.

"Whatever you have got to say, don't bother. There had better not be any trouble, now get out. Annual Summer Ball, my arse."

Much to CI Bagley's disappointment, the event passed without incident. I remember that Billy Miller served up some tasty cheese and onion rolls. Sadly, that was the last Beat Officers Summer Ball. A year later, the Government amended the licensing laws to allow all-day drinking.

On 11 June, Margaret Thatcher defeated Neil Kinnock's Labour Party, winning a historic third consecutive General Election, albeit with a slightly reduced majority.

There was a change of leadership at Kings Heath police station. Superintendent Erica Norton took over the reins and was a breath of fresh air. Believing theirs was the only opinion that mattered, most senior officers dictated policy. That was not how Erica Norton operated. She tapped into everyone's experience and ability. Supt Norton invited everyone to contribute, ensuring decisions were unanimous and transparent. She was naturally bubbly, and I liked her. At one meeting, my contribution was a little barbed. She warned me, "PC Smith, you need to be careful. You have a tongue so sharp you will cut yourself with it one day." She was right, and I did so on many occasions.

As someone who had never attended Bramshill Police College, I was oblivious to management buzzwords and expressions. Superintendent Norton suggested to a group of beat officers that deploying a van patrol on Friday or Saturday nights might be a good idea. I wasn't bothered, so I mentally drifted away from the debate. I was usually quick enough to contribute if put on the spot. The room went quiet, and Superintendent Norton asked, "What do you think, Vince? Shall we suck it and see?"
Well, that woke me up. I was shocked and embarrassed. That sentence had only ever been said to me once before, and it had nothing to do with police van patrol policy. I spluttered,

"That sounds good to me, ma'am." The Superintendent deployed a public order van on Saturday evenings. A few weeks later, she offered to "Run something up my flagpole and see if it would fly." I mentally decoded the message, removing any sexual connotation.

Mark Blackburn popped into Kings Heath to see Chris Warren, his old shift Inspector. When Mark walked into the Inspector's office, he was unaware that an angry Chief Superintendent, Tim Burn, was sitting opposite Chris. Mr Burn had just left the custody suite, where he had confronted Felix O'Neill and told him to fasten the top button of his police shirt. Burn said Sergeant O'Neil had almost strangled himself to death in a failed attempt to comply with his instruction.

The Chief Super told Warren to get a grip of his staff or else. Chris was past caring and allowing the bollocking to wash over him. Disappointed that his words had so little impact, the Chief Super asked. "Inspector Warren, is this officer one of yours?"

"Mark used to be, but he now works on a beat in Moseley." Burn turned to Mark Blackburn,

"Right then, constable, do something useful, two cups of tea, one sugar in each. And be quick about it." Chris looked a bit embarrassed.

Mark returned, placed two cups on the desk, and asked, "Will there be anything else, gents?"

"No, thanks, Mark," said Chris. The Chief Super dismissed Mark with a wave.

A couple of hours later, Mark saw that Chris Warren was in his office alone. Chris apologised to Mark for how he was spoken to earlier.

"It's okay, boss, don't worry about it. Anyway, I wiped my bell-end around the rim of his cup." Chris Warren exploded with laughter but then had a thought.

"How did you know which was his cup?"

"I didn't, so I gave both cups the same treatment. Sorry."

"Thanks a lot," Said Chris as he lit a cigarette, hoping the nicotine would kill any germs that Mark Blackburn's todger had left.

Peter attended Ulverley school in Olton, and conveniently, it was only a couple of hundred yards from home. The area was decent, and so were the kids. I was concerned that Peter's hearing could affect his progress and development. Thankfully, Peter's ears were not a problem, but I had concerns about other matters.

Peter's school report indicated that he was average in everything. I chatted with other parents. Most said their child was also average in all subjects. The school reports appeared to be generic.

My son's form teacher, Mrs Castro, went on strike as often as possible, supporting local and national teaching unions and any teaching organisation protesting anywhere on the planet. The school sports day was the final straw. I enjoyed sports days as a kid, but this was something else. There were no competitive races. The children held hands and walked to the finish line. Then they applauded each other. The headmaster's view was that competition was unfair. My view was that life was unfair.

St Andrews, a Roman Catholic school, was also close by. Their only requirement was that their children had to be Catholic.

I made an appointment to see Frank Lambert, the headmaster of St Andrews. Hundreds of photographs of pupils in their sports kit were on the wall outside his office. Most kids were holding a trophy aloft.

Next to every child was a bursting with pride, Mr Lambert.

I confirmed that Peter was Catholic. Mr Lambert said I could change schools once I had let his current school know, so I made an appointment to see Mr Moore.

Word of my intention had reached Mr Moore's ears. He told me Peter was a bright child and moving him could be a big mistake. I insisted that Peter was average at everything, and every report his school had provided confirmed that assessment. He looked a bit sheepish. Mr Moore shook my hand and wished Peter all the best. I told him that I hoped none of the children at his school ever broke ranks and tried to win a race on sports day. He winced.

Peter started at St Andrew's school. His school reports were a lot more detailed. On school sports day, every child tried to win a medal. A parent's race was the final event. While competitively eyeing up their opposition, some parents swapped their footwear for running spikes. Sports Day was so different to Peter's previous school.

I read Peter the Hobbit by JRR Tolkien, and we saw the play at the Alex Theatre in Redditch, which he loved. He started reading the Lord of the Rings. Pretty impressive for an eight-year-old. Peter had a spelling test every week, and I was disappointed that the best he could achieve was eight out of ten. I broached him. Pete smiled and said that immediately after the test, his class had playtime. Peter said the kids who achieved ten out of ten didn't fare too well in the playground. I remember thinking things were going to work out for him.

I listened to Peter talk about his teachers, particularly his form teacher, Mr Foxon. He was picking on my son for all manner of minor infractions, and Peter needed me to sort him out. I decided that the showdown would take place on parents' evening.

Fully briefed by my son, I attended parents' evening. I sat on one of the tiny chairs you can only find in a junior school. Sitting down was easy. It was getting up that I was more concerned about.

Mr Foxon was intelligent and confident. He told me what he thought about my son, which was not exactly flattering. He described Peter as a very clever boy who spent every day calculating the minimum amount of work he should produce. He added that he would not allow this to continue.

While Foxon was talking, I looked at some of Pete's work on his desk. I saw a project on the next desk marked B, and I thought it was rubbish. Peter's work had been assessed as a D for the same project and looked pretty good. I now had clear evidence of Foxon's unwarranted persecution of my child. I interrupted him, "For God's sake, you gave this kid a B for this dross. Yet Peter gets a D for this. Would you care to explain yourself?" I held up both pieces of work.

"Mr Smith, the girl who produced that, worked on it for hours. She could not have tried any harder. Peter completed his in about twenty minutes. Mr Smith, I reward effort and the standard of their work. Peter has massive potential <u>if</u> he starts working. But I fear he will achieve nothing if he continues as he is."

As I walked home, I thought about what Mr Foxon had said. Peter asked if I had sorted out Foxon. I said, "Sadly, Mr Foxon has seen through your little act. He needs you to start grafting before it's too late, and I have to say I agree with him."

On reflection, I am ashamed to say that Peter's attitude to school mirrored my approach to my job.

I knew my area very well. The sergeants and the beat officers changed, but I remained, mostly because I had nowhere else to go. Rumours about boundary and personnel changes were spread by those who would not be affected and revelled in some shit-stirring. Then, out of the blue, Woodbridge Road transferred to the Belgrave Road subdivision, and as a part of the fixtures and fittings, I moved with it.

On 16 December 1988, a fat thief masquerading as a Chief Inspector at Belgrave Road confirmed that my ten-year connection with Kings Heath had ended. I thought I coped pretty well and moved without any fuss. My police record tells a different story. I reported unfit for duty as I had vomiting and diarrhoea - I was sick of being shit on.

CHAPTER 13

CATS, PROSTITUTES AND A SPACEMAN

I returned to work on 3 January 1989. I started at Edward Road with a new team of officers, different supervision and a fixed shift pattern. Management deployed teams and moved away from individual beat responsibility. The police force loved an acronym and bestowed the title CAT's - to our Community Action Team.

It felt strange to leave Kings Heath. The area had felt like a comfortable old coat that fitted snugly. After ten years, I knew the police officers, criminals and the terrain. There was no leaving party or farewells. Worst of all, it was not my choice, so I was back at the first square on a police career Snakes and Ladders board.

I knew most of the officers at Edward Road and was delighted that my good friend Brian Bridgewater was there.

CAT's worked as a team throughout the week but covered for the shift every Thursday and worked 6am-2pm. I couldn't drive a panda car, so I was posted to the front office at Woodbridge Road. That meant a 5.30am start, so it was time to get my push bike out, pump up the tyres and spray WD 40 on the gears and brakes. With no prospect of ever driving, I thought this posting would continue until my retirement.

Management deployed our team to address cannabis dealers, prostitutes and public order situations. In addition, we policed the football, cricket, and rugby matches in Birmingham.

One night, our team received a two-minute briefing from a detective, "My snout reckons that a drugs mule will be travelling from Liverpool tonight with a rucksack full of gear. Once his train arrives, I will give you his description. Then you lot can arrest him as he walks out of the train station."

At 11pm, we parked outside New Street's train station. As the City drifted to sleep, the only sound that interrupted the silence was the station platform announcer, "The train now arriving at platform seven is the…"

We waited for hours. There was no update from the detective.

"The train now departing platform three is the…"

By 3am, but for the station announcer, I think we would all have been fast asleep.

At 4am, it was deathly silent, then Gareth Lewis, at the back of the van, cupped his hands around his mouth and, in a pitch-perfect impression of the station announcer, blared out, "The train now arriving at platforms one, two, three, four and five is fucking coming in sideways."

The van erupted. The drug baron never showed up, and we stood down.

Our team dealt with prostitutes, which was not exactly challenging. We watched a woman soliciting motorists for twenty minutes, then arrested her for prostitution. Following her charge, the custody sergeant bailed her to appear before the courts. The Magistrates usually fined the ladies a nominal amount.

One day, a solicitor representing his client pointed out that by taking money from prostitutes, the Government was living off immoral earnings. Fines ceased, and the magistrates issued supervision orders, community service and suspended sentences. To add insult to injury, if a woman had two prostitution convictions, a caution and a charge sufficed, she was referred to in court as a *common prostitute*.

Management decided that officers should report punters for soliciting a woman for the purposes of prostitution, which made the police, prostitute and punter interaction much more entertaining and created all sorts of drama. Drivers grabbed an A-Z and perused it as the officer tapped his car window. On inspection, the officer was able to challenge, "So, in the middle of Balsall Heath, you have asked this young lady for directions. Just how is a street map of Bloxwich going to assist?" The ladies found this hilarious. They had already been paid and had no loyalty to their customers.

We found it effective to allow the punter to negotiate and collect the prostitute. Then, drive her to the car park, wasteland or their romantic setting of choice. Allow them five minutes to get warmed up. Then, we formally introduced ourselves in a pincer movement similar to the one used in the film *Zulu*. This tactic usually resulted in less dialogue and drama.

Two of our team pounced on a well-known prostitute who had been picked up by a male driver. Though the officers had watched the car for ten minutes, the steamy windows had reduced visibility. The officers knocked on the car windows, and the prostitute and a middle-aged man alighted from the vehicle. The driver was wearing a particularly prominent religious dog collar. Anita, the prostitute, was arrested. The man in the dog collar announced that he was a Methodist Minister. Explaining he had only pulled over to speak to the prostitute and point out the error of her lifestyle choice.

His story might have worked if Anita had not started sniggering. The Vicar announced he was a close personal friend of the Chief Constable. For refusing to give his details, under the provisions of Section 25 of the Police and Criminal Evidence Act, he accompanied Anita to Belgrave Road police station. His final threat at the scene, "You will all be looking for new jobs in the morning. Harumph."

At the police station, I sat in the holding area with Anita. Two officers escorted the minister to an interview room to obtain his details. I could hear his loud protests about his treatment. Anita said, "You don't have any evidence against him, do you?"

"Not really."

Anita smiled and asked, "Would you like some?"

"Anita, if you are just going to tell me that you are a prostitute, and he is a punter…"

"No, I am talking about actual evidence, you divvy. Do you want some?"

"At this time, that would be very much appreciated."

"When the officers knocked on his car window, I was giving him what we call in the trade a 'posh wank'. You know, tossing him off while he was wearing a condom."

"What's your point, Anita?"

"He is still wearing the condom." She was laughing.

I put on a pair of rubber gloves, entered the interview room and seized 'Exhibit A' from the penis of an incredibly apologetic Methodist Minister. The Lord works in mysterious ways.

Our team also dealt with the local cannabis dealers. Again, this was not difficult. The dealers stood on a street corner, often amicably sharing the junction with prostitutes. After all, they offered different products/services, so they were not in competition.

Witnessing a drug deal and attempting to arrest the dealer for supply and the buyer for possession often became a farce of *Benny Hill* proportions. The purchasers were often students, identifiable by their university scarves and non-Birmingham accents. Having paid £5 for their cannabis, as the police approached, they simply swallowed the evidence. Digestion was a perfectly acceptable method of taking the drug. Without any evidence, they had no case to answer.

Drug dealers had a different dilemma. Depending on the amount of cannabis they had, swallowing the evidence may not be an option. The dealers were usually younger and fitter than the police officers. So, with a Linford Christie blast of speed, they disappeared. Leaving the police officer with a grinning student, no dealer and no evidence. The only consolation for the officer was that the student would develop a severe case of the *munchies* in a few hours. We needed to up our game.

Spaceman was a drug dealer who operated in Moseley village. He was 6' 4" and in his sixties. Spaceman sported black horn-rimmed glasses and a grey goatee beard. To make himself stand out even more, as if that was possible, he wore a green Eskimo hat with the flaps out. Spaceman offered drugs to everyone who crossed his path, even uniformed police officers on patrol. Selling cannabis was what he did, and he had a lot of customers.

On Friday evenings at 6pm, Spaceman stood outside a well-known Moseley pub, which I may or may not have been barred from previously, offering cannabis resin.

Arresting Spaceman for possession was easy. No matter how much cannabis he had in his possession, given his fraggled state, he argued that it was for personal use - resulting in a slap on the wrist at the magistrate's court. Our team set up an operation to collect evidence of Spaceman supplying cannabis.

One Friday night, Spaceman started dealing at 6pm. I wrote evidence logs and liaised with the team via radio while secreted in the attic of a curry house overlooking the pub's entrance. Those who purchased drugs and turned left remained in Spaceman's line of sight, so I ignored them. Purchasers who headed towards Moseley village were in play.

Spaceman's customers were university students. Some who made a purchase popped the drugs into their mouth. To be swallowed if the police showed an interest. I ignored those as well. I focused on purchasers who pocketed the drugs and walked towards Moseley Village.

The restaurant's owner was fascinated by the police operation and brought me samosas and shish kebabs, which were delicious. Between courses, I called the strike on several young men,

"Male, in his twenties wearing a red bobble hat, 'Frankie says Relax' T-shirt, his purchase is in the front left pocket of his jeans." My job was easy as no two students looked or dressed the same. With six drug purchasers detained and their cannabis seized, we had all the evidence we needed, and I was stuffed. Spaceman was arrested and transported to Belgrave Road police station. I thanked the restaurant owner for his assistance and hospitality.

At the station, I interviewed Spaceman, who denied committing any offences. He refused to describe himself, so I did. I only got as far as his grey goatee beard. Spaceman halted proceedings with a howl. "It is not a goatee beard!" I insisted that it was, and he shouted,

"Officer, it is not a goatee beard. It is a human beard."

"Would you agree that it's grey?"

"Officer, it's grey all over my face, all over my chest and all over my bollocks."

Spaceman was charged, pleaded not guilty on his first court appearance, and opted for trial at Birmingham Crown Court.

When a prisoner was arrested, with the authority of the Duty Inspector, officers searched their home for further evidence. This was new, and many officers thought it a waste of time, so the searches were lacklustre. Several officers on our team had more than ten years in the job, and this procedure fell neatly into their "What a load of bollocks" category.

When Sergeant Rod Bevan turned up to supervise, he often recovered a Polaroid camera. The change in application and effort of the search team was incredible. Officers dismantled floorboards, mattresses and lofts. I think Rod carried that camera around in his kit bag. There are probably several uses for a Polaroid camera other than taking naughty pictures. But to be honest, I cannot think of any.

During searches, an officer's little bit of theatre often protected the informant. For example, if the information was that there was a stash of drugs hidden in the vacuum cleaner, after a negative search, a conversation between officers, "Vinnie, is it worth checking the vacuum cleaner, just in case?"

"Might as well while we are here." Bingo.

Having decided to defend himself at trial, Spaceman was a forlorn figure. Four police officers had given evidence, and the prosecution barrister had presented a reasonably airtight case to the jury.

Spacemen interrupted proceedings by declaring, "I have a God-given right to sell cannabis on the streets!" Which annoyed the judge.

Spaceman left the dock to conduct his defence. The judge asked Spaceman if he intended to give evidence. After a pause, he answered, "There is something I need to do first, sir."

Spaceman walked towards the jury, who sat silently in two rows of six. What was he doing? The jury is an anonymous group that does not interact with any of the active participants of a trial. Their only responsibility is to deliver a verdict.

Spaceman approached the first juror, who edged away. Spaceman whispered into the juror's ear. When no response came, he shrugged, then moved on to the next juror and whispered into her ear. The judge shouted across his court, "What the hell do you think you are doing, man?"

"Judge, I am asking the jurors if they think I'm guilty. If they all do, I will change my plea." The judge warned Spaceman and ignored the sniggering police officers at the back of his court. Struggling to keep his temper, the judge instructed Spacemen to remain seated for the remainder of his trial.

Confirming the defendant would not give evidence, the case concluded in double-quick time. The judge delivered a somewhat biased summary to the jury, who retired to consider their verdict.

They returned within fifteen minutes and convicted Spaceman of supplying cannabis. Unable to hide his delight, the judge sentenced him to two years in prison. A bewildered Spaceman was transported to a galaxy not that far away called HMP Birmingham.

Peter was doing well at school, so I gave him a fatherly chat to keep him on the straight and narrow. "Pete, my Superintendent, spoke to one of my mates at work today. My friend's son, who is about your age, had been arrested for shoplifting and had to leave work to attend a police station. It was a bit embarrassing. I hope you never put me in that position." Pete stared at me or, to be more accurate, straight through me, then said, "Dad, I'm not stupid, so please don't make up any more stories. It just makes you look ridiculous." It is not great when your nine-year-old son is more intelligent than you.

CHAPTER 14

THE TIMES THEY ARE A-CHANGING

Even though I had taken to driving the way a duck takes to bricklaying, I was able to bluff my way through my DVLA driving test.

When I was qualified to drive, Hughie called me and said he had a Renault 20, which I could have for £500. I took the car to a garage on Woodbridge Road to give it a once over. I asked for an estimate for whatever work was needed to make the car road worthy. The mechanic said it would cost at least £1,700, which might not be enough. I phoned Hughie,

"Hughie, that car you have offered me is a wreck. It will cost a fortune to get it on the road. I will drop it back to you, mate."

"Wolfie, the thing is…everybody gets ripped off when they buy their first car. Why should you be any different?" I put the phone down

I purchased a 'T' reg two-door Vauxhall Cavalier with 90,000 miles on the clock, making my journey to work a lot easier. I applied for a one-day police driving course.

Between 1986 and 1990, Birmingham hosted the F3000 Super Prix. It took place over the August Bank Holiday. For the most part, I managed to avoid the event. I had no interest in motor car racing, though many officers were desperate not to miss it.

In 1989, I was selected to police the event; unusually, I could not wriggle out of it. Apologies to the Super Prix fans amongst you, but it was a noisy, petrol-fumed, smelly nightmare. The race was a blur, like watching a giant toy Scalextric. Ironically, that area is now "A Clean Air Zone."

On Saturday, 4 November 1989, Hughie McGowan, Mark Blackburn, and I travelled on a police coach to Twickenham. The coach was packed, and we had tickets to see Mark Linnett, our colleague, making his England International debut, playing prop against the touring Fiji team.

The West Midlands police had shrewdly negotiated access to the bar facilities at the Royal Military School of Music, Kneller Hall, adjacent to and only a ten-minute walk from Twickenham.

On arrival, the duty officer boarded the coach and checked our police warrant cards. He advised us that our warrant cards must be carried at all times. He made only one announcement - There was no dress code for the NAAFI bar, but there was for the sergeant's mess. Drinking would be relaxed, less crowded and far cheaper than in any local pub.

I had bought a leather jacket, and I thought it went nicely with my shirt and tie. In the sergeant's mess, I was challenged by the duty sergeant before I could take a sip from my first pint of lager. "Sir, leather jackets are not acceptable attire in this sergeant's mess. I will have to ask you to leave."

The duty sergeant pointed to the door. I looked for support from Mark and Hughie, who were enjoying their pints and waving me goodbye.

In a massive sulk, I returned to the police coach. The coach driver was a bubbly guy called Barbados. He was drinking coffee from a flask and had a plastic Tupperware box full of sandwiches on his lap. Barbados wore a maroon nylon blazer that must have cost less than £2. I shared my predicament and asked if I could borrow his jacket to return to the sergeant's mess.

He thought for a minute and made me a non-negotiable offer. The loan of my coat, plus I had to leave all his stuff in his jacket. I agreed and put on his 'cheap as chips' maroon blazer. His lead-weighted glasses case dangled near my knee. The multi-coloured display of ballpoint pens in the breast jacket pocket was the stand-out feature of the garment. I set off to re-join Hughie and Mark.

I entered the sergeant's mess and ordered a pint of lager. The same duty sergeant who had asked me to leave made a beeline for me. "Hello again, sir and first of all, I must say that jacket really suits you, and you look a lot smarter. Enjoy your afternoon." We both knew that was bollocks, but this was the British Army, and rules are rules.

Whilst the match was supposed to be a friendly, it was anything but. England won an attritional game 58-23. Two Fijian players were sent off, and the English second-row Paul Ackford was carried off. The highlight, for me, was Mark Linnett's try. Well done, mate.

In May 1990, Hughie McGowan and Yvonne Kelly decided to tie the knot and asked me to be their best man. Their wedding day was also Peter's tenth birthday.

On the morning of the wedding, I filled my car's engine with oil up to the top of the rocker box. Using the principle that if a bit of oil is good for a car's engine, a lot must be much better. Half a mile into the journey, my car's exhaust produced a trail of smoke of Batmobile proportions. I had to get a taxi to the church.

Father Pat was the Catholic priest who performed the marriage ceremony. Sadly, it was the last time he presided over any religious service. He had not lost his faith; he fell in love with a nun from a local Catholic school and eloped.

As we left the Church, guests arrived for the following wedding ceremony. Father Pat told Hughie and Yvonne the next couple could not afford flowers. Hughie and Yvonne kindly left their flowers in situ.

Hundreds of Hughie's and Yvonne's family and friends were at the reception at the West Midlands Police social club, Tally Ho. Making a speech in front of a crowd of that size was daunting, so I didn't drink until after my speech. After which, I changed out of my sweat-soaked shirt and launched myself into the festivities. I don't think any video evidence exists to contradict me, so I will say my best man speech was brilliant.

Chris Stapleton, the licensee of the Castle and Falcon, arranged and played the music at the wedding.

When Tally Ho closed, we joined Chris at his pub to continue drinking. Chris was playing his guitar when, through pure exhaustion, he fell asleep. His wife Monica slid the guitar from Chris and seamlessly continued with the song on her Irish flute. Absolute class. Hughie and Yvonne, I am delighted to say, are still happily married.

Though she didn't know it, Margaret Thatcher was about to embark on her final battle as Prime Minister. She decided to do away with the system of rates that had been in place for years and replace it with - The Poll Tax.

The British public was not happy and took to the streets to protest. While the riots in London attracted the media's attention, the council house in Birmingham also came under attack.

With hundreds of other police officers, I escorted protesters marching around the centre of Birmingham while they chanted anti-government and anti-Thatcher insults. One of the protesters asked me what I thought about the Poll Tax. "Mate, it's hard for me to offer an opinion."

"Why not? Everybody knows that it's a fucking disgrace."

"Well, that might be the case, but Mrs Thatcher has decided that police officers are exempt, I don't really have an opinion."

The protester almost choked. Struggling to contain his anger, he charged off towards the protest organisers.

Half an hour later, I saw the same guy. He was fighting with four police officers who were struggling to detain him. Eventually, they handcuffed and deposited him into the back of a police van. Police officers were not exempt from paying the Poll Tax - no one was. I felt pretty guilty.

Having won three General Elections, the Iron Lady embarked on a fourth campaign. No longer at the peak of her powers, cabinet members and dissenting Tories she would previously have crushed attacked her and would not go away. The Labour Party and the public were relentless, and Maggie could not survive. She struggled, but her demise was inevitable. Margaret Thatcher resigned on 22 November 1990.

The Conservative Cabinet minister who surgically assassinated and then replaced Maggie was the grey man John Major. He landed the British Prime Minister's job and had an affair with Edwina Currie. I can see the appeal of being PM, but I am unsure about the attraction to Mrs Currie.

In April 1991, I met up with Chris Taylor at Woodbridge Road. An instructor from the police driving school took us out for a 'one-day' test, and a pass would allow us to drive panda cars.

First up was Chris, who sat behind the wheel and drove us into the City Centre. I took over and negotiated the return journey to Woodbridge Road.

Chris and I sat in the back of his vehicle at Woodbridge Road. I don't know what I expected, marks out of ten, pass or fail, maybe advice.

The examiner was outside his car smoking. When he finished his fag he stubbed it out against a wall and climbed into his car. He turned to face Chris and me. "Right, listen in, you pair of jokers. That was the worst display of driving I have seen in thirty years as a driving instructor. As for you, Smith, I am amazed we got back alive. That cigarette you just saw me smoke was the first I have had in twenty years and was entirely your fault, Smith."

He continued, "It was like watching someone driving in the dodgems at a fairground. My nerves are shattered, but I have only a few months left doing this job. I may live to regret this, but I will award you both a pass. Stay below the speed limit, drive carefully and never forget how fucking useless at driving you are. I do not expect to see either of you on a driving course."

Even though it sounded harsh, I was absolutely delighted. On patrol, as instructed, I drove a panda car that never travelled faster than 30mph.

Around this time, Mr Foxon phoned and asked me to attend Peter's school. I feared the worst. I always did. Mr Foxon asked if I had considered Peter taking entrance exams for private schools such as Solihull School or King Edwards in Edgbaston. He said that the exams were free, but the competition was fierce. Mr Foxon suggested using a private tutor to assist and also have an independent assessment. I asked, "If Peter is as clever as you say, why does he need extra tuition?"

"Because the tests include subjects not taught at this school."

He recommended Mr Maund, a retired teacher who lived near Solihull and gave me his details. I had a lot to think about.

King Edwards and Solihull schools had the same admission criteria, two entrance exams, and a further exam to qualify for a scholarship. I booked Peter ten one-hour lessons with Mr Maund, which cost £100.

After Peter's final lesson, while Peter waited in my car, Mr Maund invited me into his house. I asked, "Well, what do you think?"

"Peter is bright and quick with his answers. I am confident he will do well in the exams. I will, however, add a cautionary note. As the standard of competition is unknown, Peter could be the cleverest boy ever, not to be offered a place."

I explained the situation to Peter, who took it in his stride. The entrance exams took place over three weekends, followed by the scholarship exams.

When I dropped Peter off at King Edwards school for his first exam, he looked nervous and clutched his pencil case. As I drove off, I wound down my window and called, "Peter, fail this exam, and you are out of the family."

Peter thought he had done okay in the exams but was grateful for Mr Maund's help. He said the maths papers contained questions about binary, which he could only answer because of Mr Maund's tuition. I nervously waited while Peter just waited.

Mr Jennings, my Superintendent, was a pompous snob, and we did not mix in the same social circles. I did not own a university scarf, whereas Jennings wore his whatever the weather.

I was on duty at the Reddings and saw Mr Jennings and his scarf. He was chatting to a couple of Moseley committee members. I tried and failed to avoid him. "Ah, PC Smith, can I have a quick word."

"What can I do for you, sir?"

"Can you attend my office on Monday at 9.30am?"

"Of course, I can, sir, no problem. In fact, as it happens, I need to speak to you about something."

He looked puzzled. I had batted the ball back to him. As I walked away, he said, "Actually, Smith, I have a few minutes now if that is any good."

"That's okay, sir. Monday will be fine."

I did not attend his office on Monday. I knew he was showboating.

A mate told me that Jennings had two boys at Solihull School, and the school fees were crippling him.

A few weeks later, I saw Jennings sitting at his desk. His brow was creased, and he appeared to be wrestling with a problem. If I had to guess, it would have been about the parking in the police station yard. It was a perennial problem - how to allocate another inch or two to his personal parking space.

"Sir, do you have a couple of minutes? I could do with some advice regarding a private matter."

"Yes, but it can only be a couple of minutes. I have an important meeting to attend." When didn't they?

"Fine, sir, I will not keep you long. What do you think of Solihull Boys private school?"

He sat up and, for some reason, picked up a pencil.

"PC Smith, do you have a private income, or are your family particularly wealthy?"

"No, to both, sir."

"What does your wife do for a living?"

"She's a part-time nurse, sir."

He stared at his pencil, smiled and then said so slowly I could tell he was enjoying this,

"Firstly, Solihull School is an amazing educational institution. I have two sons there, and brilliant though it is, you could never afford the fees."

He sat back and soaked up my disappointment. Then asked, "Will there be anything else?"
I stood to leave and said, "But would you recommend the school, sir?"
Frustrated, he said, "You haven't heard a single bloody word…"

"Sir, my son has received the offer of a full scholarship at Solihull School. So it will not cost me a penny." As I walked out of his office, I heard a pencil snap.

Peter was offered a full scholarship at Solihull School and a partial scholarship at King Edwards. As the school was much closer, we accepted Solihull's offer. Peter was a little disappointed. JRR Tolkien had attended King Edwards, and Peter would have loved to have followed in his footsteps.

When Peter's large acceptance letter arrived, I searched through it, looking for a financial catch. If there were no school fees, there must be something that would cost me money apart from the expensive uniform. I found it. Every child on admission identified an instrument and received ten musical assessment lessons at a cost of £100. I made a note to cancel Peter's music lessons as soon as possible.

Inspector Helen Willetts was put in charge of the Community Action Team. I was unceremoniously dumped onto D Unit at Belgrave Road. Though I was gutted at the time, looking back, it was the best thing that ever happened to me. So thank you, ma'am.

CHAPTER 15

ONE STEP BACK TWO STEPS FORWARD

D Unit at Belgrave Road was much busier than Kings Heath or Moseley. With over ten years in the job, I was able to cope. Inspector Phil Walsh was in charge of my shift. He worked hard and expected the same from his troops.

We had some talented Zulu drivers on the shift, Mair Poyner, who, when it was quiet, tootled around like a lady out on a Sunday afternoon jaunt. Then, when required, she hit the accelerator and gears like a Formula 1 racing driver. Paul Gwinnett was an accomplished 'Hill Climb' competitor, driving his race car without a speedometer. I assumed he judged his speed by how quickly the wind blew through his hair. Bob Holland was an experienced driver and also a qualified glider pilot.

Bob took my son on a flight from the airfield at Bidford-on-Avon. Pete loved the experience and never forgot it. Thank you, Bob.

Whenever the shift turned out for an immediate response, I was one of the first to charge out of the station and jump into the passenger seat of a police car. Leaving my panda car keys in the station ensured I would not be driving to wherever we went.

Phil Walsh decided to broaden my horizons with or without my consent. He accepted that my driving was beyond redemption, so we didn't go there. He identified the role of sub-division controller as my next challenge. He told me, "That's an area of police work you will not be able to bluff your fucking way through."

I usually just went through the motions during police courses. As far as I was concerned, it was a bunch of waffling trainers who loved the sound of their own voices. This course lasted fourteen days. We started at 8am and finished at 3pm. Two types of messages landed on the controller's screen - High Priority and Routine. If too many high priorities were outstanding, alarms were triggered in the Force Control Room, and the telephone line to the controller became extremely busy. Ignored routine messages could escalate into high priorities.

I was determined to soak up as much information as possible. I knew I would be on my own if something serious happened at 4am while working nights. There was a pass-or-fail exam on the last day.

I returned to Belgrave Road, qualified to sit in the controller's chair. Mr Walsh posted me as a controller for weeks at a time. I can't say it was enjoyable, but it kept me focused, and I saw another side to policing. My keyboard skills improved, which helped. For eight hours, I gazed at a consul with green type that blinked. I must have done okay as I received the occasional nod from Inspector Walsh.

On my behalf, Peter delivered a letter to his school, cancelling his piano lessons. The same night, the Headmaster, Mr Alan Lee, phoned me and acknowledged receipt of my letter. When he asked me why I wished to cancel my son's piano lessons, I had prepared my response, "Mr Lee, my son has no musical ability whatsoever. In fact, for generations, there has not been anyone in my family who could even whistle."

"Mr Smith, are you aware that your son can read and play music?"

After only ten lessons, I found that hard to believe. We didn't even have an instrument in the house. I put Mr Lee on hold, then tiptoed upstairs to Peter's bedroom.

"Can you read music?"

"Yes, Dad."

"Can you play music?"

"I can play a keyboard."

"Where the hell have you learned to do that?

"Next door."

Our neighbours were Polish, and the Dad had one of those Wurlitzer organs usually only found in a 1930s cinema.

"Are you any good?"

"Fairly good." Wrong answer.

I returned to the phone, "Sorry to keep you waiting, Mr Lee, but something had just come up. I think that some wires have become crossed. Of course, Peter will continue with his music lessons for the foreseeable future."

That weekend, I purchased a Casio keyboard. Pete eventually achieved a Grade 4 (Piano) in music.

I bought a second-hand set of golf clubs, owned a car, and took up golf. I played several rounds at the local municipal courses and enjoyed the challenge. The best private golf course I played was Moseley. I made some enquiries and discovered that several Freemasons were club members. Though not a mason, I ensured both my proposers were. My application was successful. Thank you, Dean Baxter and Jim Ashmore.

Not wishing to punctuate this book with repeated visits into my golfing voyage, here are my highlights.

I was an active member at Moseley Golf Club for ten years, playing in weekly tournaments. I chipped away at my club handicap. My lowest handicap was eight. I had three holes-in-one in local and national competitions.

In 1993, I won the West Midlands police handicap tournament, beating one hundred and thirty other entrants. Moseley Golf Club hosted the competition, which gave me a slight advantage.

At the presentation dinner, Martin Yates, an Inspector I worked with, tapped me on the shoulder, "Well done, Wolfie. I've watched you play from when you first started. You had a golf swing that looked like an octopus falling out of a window. I never thought you could win a tournament like this." I suppose that was a sort of back-handed compliment.

I once qualified for the National Police Golf tournament at Walton Heath and had one of my holes-in-one at the 17th hole on the Old Course.

Most years, I qualified for the Regional Police Golf Championships at Little Aston, Warwickshire - a superb course with an incredibly posh clubhouse. It was a 36-hole competition. After the first 18 holes, the club provided soup and sandwiches. Clubhouse rules required a jacket (not leather) and tie to be worn. One hundred and forty participants wore jackets with a police uniform clip-on tie. Though not sartorially elegant, we complied with the rules.

I never played well at Little Aston and was just glad to qualify for the event. After an exhausting 36 holes, the players sat down for a meal. The guest of honour was Peter Joslin, the Chief Constable of Warwickshire. He was not a golfer and only attended to sample the excellent wine offered by the Golf Club. As a Chief Constable, he had a driver, so he did not even attempt to moderate the amount he drank.

A senior officer from the West Midlands usually bullied a constable into saying grace before the meal. He enjoyed selecting a shy officer, or better still, one with a stammer. One year, a slightly squiffy Mr Joslin interjected, pulled rank and insisted that he would say grace.

"Gentlemen, please stand up." He continued, "Lord, we respectfully ask you to help those of us who require assistance in our daily battle with alcohol. We also request that you help the weak-willed married officers amongst us to stop chasing fallen and loose women. Lord, we ask for your help with both of these issues...But Lord, not just yet."

My biggest regret was that I stopped playing when my life and work became busy. When I retired in 2014, I thought I could dust off my clubs and continue where I had left off. I couldn't. Physically, nothing worked, and my swing resembled a dead octopus falling out of a second-floor window. I took up Scrabble.

On 2 December 1992, Harold Smith (71), Mary Smith (72), and their disabled son Harold (47) were found dead in their small bungalow in Northfield. They had been stabbed to death in a frenzied attack. The exhibit's officer described the scene as an abattoir. The family lived a life of poverty and possessed nothing of value.

This enquiry was a Category A homicide - Where the identity of the offender(s) is not apparent, and securing evidence requires significant resource allocation.

I was one of the many resources allocated to this investigation. It was made clear to me that I was not a detective or a temporary detective. I was a uniformed police constable who was being allowed to wear his own clothes.

There were no clues or lines of enquiry. Even a reward of £5,000 for information had no impact. The local and national news was desperate for information and focused on the one hundred and forty-nine stab wounds the victims suffered.

BBC Crimewatch declined an invitation to assist. They said, "It was a bit *Spooky-Do*." Whatever that meant.

The Incident Room received a letter from a lady who claimed she had psychic powers and that if allowed to attend the scene, she would connect to the deceased and find out what had happened.

As the new kid on the block, I was selected to escort the psychic. As a natural sceptic, I was not hopeful. My fears were confirmed. I opened the front door of the bungalow, and the psychic threw herself on the floor and screamed, "Knives, knives, I can see knives!" The psychic did not provide the breakthrough that some had hoped.

I booked a visit with a colleague to see a prisoner at Ford Open Prison, as he may have overheard someone talking about the murders while he was in the cell block at Bournville Lane.

I had never worked with anyone who allowed me to drive, and my colleague that day was no different. The return journey to Ford prison was over three hundred and fifty miles. We set off at 9 am, and at the prison, I spoke to an unpleasant individual who told me to fuck off.

We returned to Woodbridge Road and managed to catch the 6pm briefing and update the team. It was time to go home. I got into my Vauxhall Cavalier and waited. Nothing. I realised what my problem was. I was sat in the front passenger seat (as I had all day). My vehicle, much like the enquiry, was going nowhere.

I learnt how incident rooms operated. During briefings, where possible, detectives briefed the SIO. If a constable dared to express their views, a top City detective would cut them short and convert their fumbling into whatever the boss wanted to hear.

After six months, repeated appeals for information produced nothing. I felt deflated. Sadly, that triple murder remains undetected.

I inadvertently caused Peter a problem by buying him a fairly expensive briefcase. When opened, it had a writing platform, which I thought Pete could use for his homework on the bus to and from school.

The bus stop to Solihull was about thirty yards from my house. That bus delivered many children to schools in Solihull. Peter was the only one attending

Solihull School and the only child carrying a briefcase. Peter's battles on the bus only occurred on the way to school, as his school hours were so long that all the other kids had arrived home by the time he set off.

"Dad, could you use my briefcase for work?"

"Don't you like it?"

"I love it, but the thing is, every other kid on the bus has a rucksack. It causes me a problem every morning. I just want to blend in, if that's okay." Pete got a rucksack, and I still have his briefcase.

In February 1993, I joined the Divisional Crime Support Unit at Edward Road. Sixteen constables, half of which were detectives. Four sergeants, two of which were detectives. A Detective Chief Inspector and a Detective Inspector managed the team. We all worked in plain clothes, which caused a problem. The substantive detectives feared, with good reason, that their superior status may not be evident to the untrained eye. Another endearing quality of the detective was that when a member of the public appeared impressed by a mere constable, then it was time to interrupt and explain the constable's lack of qualifications compared to their own impressive detective credentials.

Our Detective Inspector John 'Bosher' Pestridge, who I knew from Kings Heath, came into the office holding keys for the six new cars allocated to the Crime Unit. Everyone gathered around, and one officer pleaded. "Sir, sir, I am easily the best driver on the unit. Ask anyone." That wasn't me.

Mr Pestridge randomly threw keys around the room, and officers scrambled for them. As he knew me, he threw the last set of keys in my direction. I could not have been less interested and let the keys hit my chest and drop to the floor. A couple of officers grappled for them. I did not get involved.

The system of registering informants was pretty slack. You did not have to meet an informant. Just suggest they were *working for you*, slide their name into an envelope with their criminal record number and forward it to the Detective Chief Inspector. Create a pseudonym, and that was the job done. You could enhance your informant's status by converting tittle-tattle from around the station onto intelligence logs sourced to your grass.   Senior officers were always impressed at a briefing when a detective threw in the line, "I'll have a word with my snout boss." A detective's informant was accepted as being 'tried and tested.' Having informants, real or imagined, added status and put a noticeable spring in the step of the officer.

My sergeant was a bit of a gadget freak and bought himself a Casio digital diary. He explained its features to a hardly enthralled audience. It could store up to 5,000 telephone contacts, which was handy for an important supervisor like himself.

After a couple of days, he had input all his contact details. I waited until he went to the toilet and dinked the reset button on the back of the gadget. The display read - *press the reset button again to delete all data.* I did. Over the next month, I deleted the data on his gadget four times. He eventually sent it back to Casio as it was faulty. It wasn't.

A few months later, the same sergeant had a BT pager. It was one of those devices that you phoned a number and left either a contact number or a short message. His first two hundred messages were - 'low battery.' The bin next to his desk was full of discarded AA batteries, which he believed were faulty. The rest of us knew they weren't and used them when he was not around.

The sergeant returned the pager to BT several times, who returned it with a note confirming it was 'not faulty'. Detective Inspector Pestridge told us to knock it on the head as the sergeant was not getting any work done. Also, the admin department was querying the number of AA batteries our unit was getting through.

We were a group of officers who could be attached to an incident room. As was the case in early June 1993 when Mohammed Hanif, a 43-year-old garage attendant in Hall Green, did not return home after his shift. His family reported him missing, and they were distraught. It was the feast of Eid, and his children had waited, in vain, for their father to return so they could open their presents.

Two days later, Mr Hanif was found dead in a field in Earlswood, Warwickshire. The offenders robbed his workplace and drove Mr Hanif to Earlswood in his car. The offenders murdered Hanif and burnt out his car.

A murder incident room was set up and quickly gathered momentum. Officers from the incident room arrested two suspects within days

The pathologist stated someone had repeatedly stamped on Hanif's chest. Adding the offender was a large and physically powerful individual. Detectives searched the suspects' homes and recovered cigarettes stolen from Hanif's garage. Neither suspect spoke during their interviews.

There was a significant physical difference between the suspects. One was 6' 4" and well-built, the other 5' 8" and skinny. Even though the suspects had torched Hanif's car, it provided critical evidence. The driver's seat was set as far back as possible, and someone had adjusted the wing and rear-view mirrors to allow a 6' 4" person to drive the vehicle. Both suspects were charged and remanded in custody, and their trial was scheduled for April 1995.

Case building and CPS liaison helped to develop detectives, even if I wasn't one. To put that right, I applied to become a detective and attended an interview.

In October, my informant told me about an offender who had absconded from Birmingham's secure psychiatric facility, Reaside Clinic. He was there because he had murdered his girlfriend and, at his trial, was found not guilty by reason of insanity. My informant said the man had left the area and worryingly had moved into a flat with a young woman.

I led a team of officers to an address in Bristol. The absconder opened the door, and I arrested him. I checked that the young woman in the flat was fine, then returned the prisoner to the Reaside clinic.

That was decent police work by anyone's standards. I had a bit of a swagger as I walked around Bournville Lane police station, which didn't last long.

At 1pm, the organisation released the successful list of detective applicants. The front office staff posted a telexed copy of the list in the station Briefing Book. I read the entry a dozen times and was not on the list. It hurt. In fact, it still does.

I saw Detective Inspector Phil Walsh a few weeks later. He said,

"I heard you dipped your CID board, you tosser. Do you want to be a detective, or will you sit around moaning about life not being fair?" I told him I wanted to be a detective.

"Right, get back to work and put a shift in. You can start by studying for the sergeant's exam in March. Take it and pass it. Then get in touch with me when you have done that."

CHAPTER 16

ON THE LADDER TO PROMOTION

I returned to Edward Road and grafted. Working for Detective Sergeant Whitehouse and being partnered with Tony Taylor was testing and enjoyable.

I used everyday situations to improve my knowledge and used the Ospre promotion study books as a reference guide. Working for Derek ensured I was busy with - arrests, detention, searches, interviews and property seizure. It really helped.

On 15 March, I attended Birmingham University and sat the promotion exam. It was a two-hour paper and multiple choice. After the exam, I was confident I had passed but did not want to count my chickens.

In June, I received confirmation that I had passed Part 1 of the Sergeants exam. I reapplied to be a detective, was successful and attended a temporary detective course in October.

On 16 November, I attended West Mercia Police HQ Hindlip Hall for the second part of the promotion process, Ospre II.

I am sure it has all changed, but this was 1994. The invigilators processed fourteen students at a time. There were seven reading/preparation rooms and seven scenario rooms. Every candidate had five minutes to complete the task in each room. Then, a buzzer sounded, and the door opened. The candidate left the room and moved to the next door on the left. The buzzer sounded again a minute later, and the candidate entered the room. The process continued until the candidates had visited all fourteen rooms.

As I left Hindlip Hall, I reflected on my performance. The process was a blur, but I was glad to have had fifteen years of police experience to draw on. I had no idea how I had done. Two months later, I received confirmation that I passed the sergeant's exam and, from a national perspective, was qualified for promotion.

In April 1995, the two suspects charged with the murder of Mohammed Hanif stood trial at Birmingham Crown Court. I was about to be a witness in a murder trial, which was unknown territory to me.

Crown Court was a flurry of activity involving barristers, solicitors, CPS and police officers. I stayed out of the way of those who knew what they were doing.

The defendants offered to plead guilty to manslaughter. The CPS did not accept their offer. The murder trial got underway.

I read and re-read my pocketbook and statements. I did not relax for a second. I gave evidence and thought I performed well. The trial lasted three weeks. Neither defendant gave evidence, and the jury found both men guilty of murder. The defendants were sentenced to life imprisonment.

Three years later, in 1998, a 37-year-old paedophile was kicked to death in Long Lartin prison. The larger of the two defendants convicted of the Mohammed Hanif murder was convicted of that murder and received a further life imprisonment sentence.

I assisted the Humberside Police Force with a murder-suicide investigation. A man abducted and killed his second wife, Alena. He rolled her corpse up in a piece of carpet, which he dumped at the side of a road in Hull.

Returning to Birmingham, the murderer attended the address of his fifteen-year-old son, Joseph. He attacked Joseph with a hammer and left him for dead. The man drove back to Hull and killed himself.

The Humberside police had two dead bodies to deal with and led the inquiry. The DCI who arrived with his team was impressive. One of his officers was updating him about a witness. The DCI cut him short and said, "Give me the statement, and I will read it over a coffee."

The officer sheepishly said, "I haven't written the statement yet, sir."

The DCI slaughtered him, "I have a murder, a suicide and an attempted murder to investigate, and you want to tell me a fucking story. I deal with facts and statements. Don't ever do this again, or you will be back on a shift, son."

I was sent to Pershore Road, Birmingham, to take the statement from Joseph. At the address, a social worker ushered me into the front room. She explained the lad had autism. I had no idea what that meant. The social worker advised me to speak slower, not talk at him, smile and be patient; she acted as Joseph's appropriate adult.

Joseph remembered his father walking into his bedroom, holding a hammer and striking him six times on the head. I presumptuously asked, "Why was your father trying to kill you?" He was puzzled. I waited. "Sir, my Dad loves me. He would never try to hurt me."
Perhaps autism caused him not to connect his father's actions with his intent.

On 14 April, I met the murderer's first wife. She was required to identify her ex-husband at Hull Cemetery. I collected her at 6am. She asked if I could get her home as soon as possible. At the Coroners department, I introduced her to the pathologist. After the formal identification, we set off on the return journey. Approaching the outskirts of Birmingham, the ex-wife asked, "Are you an advanced police driver, officer?"

I wasn't, but hoping for a compliment, I said yes, adding, "Why do you ask?"

"Do you know you have not used the car's indicators since we set off first thing this morning?"

When she got out of the car, I checked the indicators, hoping they didn't work. They worked fine, and the clicking noise they made was quite loud. However, they required the driver to push the lever up or down. That journey was two hundred and seventy miles. I could hear a little voice in the back of my head…*never forget how fucking useless a driver you are.*
The Coroner had everything he needed to wrap up the enquiry.

One Sunday morning in October, I received a phone call at home. The headmaster of Solihull School spoke to me. The memory still sends a shiver down my spine. When I confirmed that Peter was at home, Mr Lee asked, "Mr Smith, drive Peter to Solihull School and get here as soon as possible." I was concerned,

"Mr Lee, can you tell me what this is about?"

"Mr Smith, there is not a second to waste."

Twenty minutes later, with several other parents and school children, I stood in the main hall with Peter. Mr Lee made his way to the stage, switched on a microphone and sombrely addressed the gathering. "Firstly, thank you all for arriving so quickly. I have some terrible news, and there is no nice way to say this. James Hoccom, a pupil from this school, died of meningitis yesterday. You are here because your children are in the same school year as James.

By lunchtime, all the children in James Hoccom's school year had received a life-saving penicillin inoculation. Sadly, that does not explain the tragic story of why James died.

In May 1996, his death was the subject of a Coroner's Inquest. The press reported -

"A coroner last night recorded an open verdict into the death of a 15-year-old boy. James Hoccom was allegedly refused life-saving treatment at a cash-starved hospital and later died from a meningitis-related disease.

The inquest heard that the 6ft 6in-tall basketball player James Hoccom, of Solihull, West Midlands, was taken to the town's hospital by his parents late on 14 October last year.

His father, Bill, a company director, said that James was a strong, healthy young man but was suffering from the flu after an outbreak at Solihull Boys' School.
His GP saw him, but his condition deteriorated, and the family suspected meningitis. When they arrived at Solihull Hospital, Mr Hoccom pleaded with a doctor to administer life-saving penicillin. As James was a paediatric case, the senior house officer who examined James said their policy was to transfer paediatric patients to the Heartlands Hospital, which was ten miles away. James arrived at the Heartlands Hospital two hours later. Despite the efforts of the medical staff, he died after collapsing at 4.30am. The Coroner, Doctor Richard Whittington, said he could find no evidence that the delay in administering antibiotics had directly caused James's death. He died as a result of a natural disease."

It is only my opinion, but I believe James Hoccom died because the hospital, for no good reason, <u>failed</u> to administer a single dose of penicillin to a dying boy aged just fifteen.

RIP James X.

One of my informants turned up at the police station with a tale to tell. He and four other men were to travel to Nairobi and return with a suitcase full of cannabis resin, for which he would receive £500. The team had treated a red suitcase to prevent the drugs from being detected by x-ray at Birmingham Airport.

My mole named the other gang members and gave me the flight times. The gang believed customs would only select one individual on their return to be searched. One of the gang of four was a loud, obnoxious Rastafarian, who the gang hoped would catch the eye of the customs officers and be selected for a search.

I completed an intelligence log and sourced it to my informant. To my untrained eye, they seemed to have thought of everything. I was looking for some corroboration of their intention. So, while the gang were in the departure lounge on their outward journey, I asked a customs officer to examine the red suitcase. He called me back and asked, "Do you know what they have done to this suitcase?"

"Not really, just that it would prevent the case from being x-rayed."

The customs guy started laughing, proper laughing. Then explained, "These clowns have put brown paper in the lining of the suitcase. Which prevents jack-shit. Are you sure they are drug smugglers, and this is not just a shit episode of *Only Fools and Horses*?"

My informant dropped out of the mission at the last minute. He told the gang that he feared that there might be a police informant involved. I suppose, in many ways, he was right.

On their return to Birmingham airport, the police arrested the gang - and seized cannabis resin, with a street value of £37,000, from their red suitcase.

At the home address of one of the suspects, I recovered a suitcase because the lining had brown paper inserted. It was supportive evidence of their activities and stupidity.

My informant was paid £50 for his trouble, which explains why he never provided information to the police again.

CHAPTER 17

"THAT'S RIGHT, FORTY MILLION"

I started work in the CID office at Belgrave Road. Detectives wore suits and ties, and aftershave was optional. I was a TDC, and the T stood for temporary. I had to complete two successful three-month attachments with two Detective Sergeants to change my title from a T to a D. There were plenty of substantive detectives around to remind me of my place in the food chain.

Subject to the Detective Inspector's approval, the CID dealt with crime prisoners left in the cells overnight. At 3am, the police arrested a young man called David Princip, who was caught breaking into a social club in Balsall Heath. Princip was in the cells waiting to be dealt with. The statement of arrest and crime papers were attached to the custody sheet. I read the documents, and everything appeared straightforward.

The custody sergeant confirmed Princip was a frequent flyer and did not want a solicitor for his interview. I thought I might be able to deal with him in double-quick time.

In the interview room, before I put the tapes in the machine, Princip said, "You fucking detectives think you're something special. Swanning around like you own the place. Well, for your information, you aren't special, but I am."

I looked at him, and he didn't look special to me. Princip smiled and continued, "Okay. How many murders would you say your family are responsible for?" I paused and replied.

"That would be a combined total of none, Mr Princip. What about yours?"

He smugly said, "In 1914, my relative Gavrilo Princip shot and killed Archduke Franz Ferdinand in Sarajevo. Which started the First World War. Forty million people died in that war. That's right forty million."

I charged Princip with burglary and remanded him in custody on behalf of the Archduke and the forty million who had died. The Encyclopedia Britannica at Kings Heath Library confirmed David Princip's claim.

After three months, my detective sergeant assessed my performance as above average. In the main, my report was glowing. She pointed out that while my humour was mostly appropriate, I got a little carried away when commenting about colleagues. She was right.

In October 1995, I started my second CID attachment. While walking through the front office on my first day, the office man said a visitor wanted to speak to a detective - well, I was only the letter 'T' away from being a proper detective.

The visitor told me his neighbour had a stash of cannabis resin. The drugs were in a Quality Street tin, on top of a Welsh dresser in his dining room. I took the details and checked them with the local intelligence officer. It looked promising. I signed the time book, went straight to the magistrate's court, and obtained a search warrant.

I met my new detective sergeant and said I had a drugs warrant, which we could execute the following morning. That never happened. This CID office had a more sedate approach to crime-fighting - one of the senior detectives apparently brought in muffins on a Tuesday.

I attended courses I had already taken, trouped off to court whether required or not and was allowed as much time off as I wanted. It was almost as if they didn't want me near their office. With the possibility of my promotion board looming, I used the time to prepare.

One job made me laugh. It was midday, and a businessman parked his BMW outside his office in Northfield. He had only popped in to pick up some papers when he heard a car window smash. He looked out of his window, and his worst fear was confirmed. He saw a skinny feral youth reaching into his car, dragging his briefcase out of a broken window and sprinting off. The quick-thinking businessman rang his mobile phone, which was in his briefcase. Though out of breath, the youth answered the phone, "What?"

"Don't hang up. You can keep the briefcase and the phone."

"I'll keep the fucking lot if I want, you prick."

"Listen, I just need the laptop in my briefcase. It has all my business contact details."

"How much?"

"I'll give you £1,000, no questions asked." There was a delay while the master criminal hatched his plan.

"Right, you have forty-five minutes. I will be in the bar of the Black Horse on the Bristol Road. I will not be hanging about. Oh, and no funny business."

The businessman had not thought about any funny business until now. After brushing the broken glass off the driver's seat, he jumped into his car and drove to Bournville Lane police station.

At the police station car park entrance, he saw two detectives. He asked them to get into his car and said he would explain en route as there was little time to spare.

At the Black Horse pub, one of the detectives went into the bar and saw a youth anxiously scanning the room. More importantly, he had a laptop tucked under his arm. The detective stepped forward and asked,

"Is that my laptop?"

"Probably. Have you got my £1,000?"

The detective reached into his jacket pocket. The thief smiled, which only lasted until the police officer produced his warrant card. The detective arrested the thief and took him to Bournville Lane.

At the station, the prisoner insisted he did not need a solicitor. The detectives inserted tapes into the tape recorder. Following introductions and legal explanations, the suspect explained that he met someone he didn't really know, who gave him a laptop and said a man in the Black Horse would hand him £1,000 for the laptop. He was going to meet the man who had given him the laptop somewhere later, but he couldn't remember where. The detectives allowed him to waffle on.

A detective confronted the suspect with the evidence, the recovered laptop, and the stolen mobile

phone he had in his pocket when arrested. The thief said,
"That isn't enough to convict me at court. What else have you got?"
"Well, there is always voice recognition."
"What the fuck is that?"
"The victim spoke to the offender, who I believe is you, while you were committing the offence."
"So what?"
"Well, we have been interviewing you for ten minutes. I will play the tape of this interview to the victim. He can compare the voice on this tape to the thief he spoke to earlier. That is called voice recognition, that is."
Silence. The thief was puzzled. Finally, the detective said,
"Is there anything you would like to say?"
In a voice best described as a cross between a Dalek and a robot, through tightly gritted teeth, he replied, *"I have nothing further to add. At this stage. Officer."* Convicted

Shortly before Christmas, my detective sergeant recommended my transfer to the CID. My sergeant wrote two pages of platitudes, cliches and banalities. Goodbye 'T'.

I was posted to Acocks Green and took up a position as a detective. I was busy on two fronts - work and promotion.
Once again, I went to see Phil Walsh. It was good to have someone I could trust in my corner, even though his delivery was blisteringly caustic. Phil

advised me to apply for a CID foundation course immediately. The promotion boards would happen, but without that course under my belt, a promotion might be a one-way ticket to a career in the custody block.

Having navigated the paper sift, and a local promotion board, my final hurdle for promotion was a central board chaired by Supt Geoff Rees. I did not know him, but I had worked with his brother John Rees on B Unit when I joined the job. We had shared a lager and fag end in the Oxford Club one night after a 2-10 shift.

My interview was scheduled to take place in Supt Rees's office at Steelhouse Lane Police Station. I devised a plan that nearly cost me any chance of promotion and my job.

I spoke to Mr Rees's secretary about the possibility of seeing him. She said he was always available. However, every day at 12.30pm he walked through the City centre for an hour and had lunch.

Perfect, I did not want to speak to Mr Rees. I just wanted to see the layout of his office. Was there a carpet I could trip over, an obscure painting, a collection of police helmets or anything that might distract me?

Two days before my interview, at 12.40pm, I entered Mr Rees's office and soaked up the surroundings. There was a window, some certificates on a wall, and a table where I assumed the panel would sit.

I had only been in the office for a few seconds, but it had put my mind at ease. I was leaving when the office door opened, and Mr Rees walked in.

"And just who the fuck are you?"

"PC Smith, sir."

"Okay, what are you doing in my office?"

"Sir, I am due to come here for a promotion board on Thursday. I have never been in this office before. I just wanted to see the layout."

"Bollocks, you are looking for the questions we will ask you on your board."

"Sir, I get nervous if I am somewhere I have never been. I only wanted to see your office before Thursday. Honest."

"Is that true?"

"Yes, sir." It was every word.

The mood in the room changed. Mr Rees stared at me while he pondered my fate - sack, arrest, cancel my promotion board, or all of the above. He mellowed, smiled and said, "I have to say your preparation is extremely thorough. Best of luck, officer. I will see you on Thursday." He shook my hand.

On 15 January 1996, I met the promotion panel. Thankfully, Mr Rees did not slip me a crippler. I could do nothing more and had to wait for the panel's decision.

It was also a busy time for Peter. He had twelve GCSEs to sit and a school that demanded results from everyone, especially its scholarship students. I let Pete get on with his studying and revision. I could not exactly help him with his Latin. I had never even met a 'Lat'.

The date for my regional CID foundation course was March 4. It was a six-week residential course at Tally Ho.

On 5 February 1996, Chief Superintendent John Carter summoned me to his office to receive the result of my promotion board. Mr Carter was all smiles, shook my hand and asked me to sit down. He said that after consideration, I would be promoted to sergeant on 19 February and take up a posting at Rose Road in Harborne. I said, "Thank you, sir, and that is great news. I am extremely grateful." I hesitated, and Mr Carter asked, "Okay, but there's a but isn't there. There is always a but."

"Sir, I have the opportunity to attend a CID foundation course on 4 March. Of course, I want a promotion, but my long-term goal is a career in criminal investigation. So my request is, can I attend the course?"

Mr Carter looked at me and said, "Sergeant, (that was a good sign) wait outside my office for five minutes, then knock on my door and come back in."

Over that year, I negotiated four hurdles for promotion and other obstacles to being a substantive detective. My fate was now in the hands of a man I had only known for a few minutes. I checked my watch and knocked on the door.

Mr Carter said, "Right, this should not take long. You will join A Unit at Rose Road on the 19 February because you have earned your promotion. I have decided to allow you to attend your CID course, after which you will return to your shift. I wish you all the very best." He stood up and gave me a firm handshake.

With a uniform posting looming, I had a problem. I never looked after my uniform, but I knew the stores kept records of issued equipment. I put the few uniform rags I owned into a small kit bag and trudged off to the stores - a modern warehouse in the city centre. Though Percy no longer featured, I was pretty sure the staff would be every bit as unhelpful. I no longer had Mark Blackburn to fight my corner. I was on my own. My prepared hard-luck stories included recent spells in plain clothes, several moves and numerous unreported locker break-ins and thefts.

Uniform stores, police and military, had a unique smell, which teased that they had loads of equipment and the shelves looked full. The question was whether I could negotiate with the staff to part with anything.

I was in a queue directly behind Dominic Kennedy. My kit bag felt incredibly light. Dom didn't have a kit bag and had been a detective for years. We knew each other because when we got drunk, we would recite poetry, mostly Rudyard Kipling, at each other. The storeman produced Dom's record of issued kit. I watched with interest. "Sergeant Kennedy, can I just inspect your uniform and equipment to assess it as either fit for purpose or confirm that it needs replacing."

"Listen, mate. I have got fuck all. It's all gone, stolen, sold, worn out or thrown out. If I tear my house to bits, I might be able to find you a glove. So basically, I need everything." The storeman looked less than impressed. He was pondering what to do next.

I kicked my kitbag under a bench. Dom turned around and said, "Yo, Wolfie didn't see you there, mate. Me and you fucking sergeants, who would believe that?"

Dom was a bit annoyed at the delay and addressed the storeman, "Mate, I am on nights at Steelhouse Lane on Monday, and at this rate, I will be parading in my fucking skid-marked grundies." The storeman chucked the list of issued kit and uniform in a bin and trotted off to relieve the shelves of some of its precious stock.

He returned and presented a small mountain of brand-new uniform to Sgt Kennedy. While Dom was gathering up his new stuff, the storeman asked me. "What can I do for you?"

"Well, it's pretty simple. What Sergeant Kennedy said also applies to me. I need everything."
The storeman revisited the shelves with an empty trolly while I glanced guiltily at my kit bag.

Following promotion, officers policed a different area. Which I thought was a good idea as it allowed a fresh start with a cleanish slate.

I attended a six-week CID Foundation course with twenty-four students from police forces around the midlands.

On the first day, Roger Crotty, the Detective Sergeant who ran the course, pulled me to one side. He explained that I was the only sergeant on the course and should be careful as many students had accidentally committed professional suicide while attending courses at Tally Ho.

The Superintendent in charge of the course met us for a meet-and-greet chat. He told us we had three weeks to prepare a project about the positive effect of the Neighbour Hood Watch schemes. A mate confided that the Chief Constable had tasked the Superintendent to investigate the impact of Neighbour Hood Watch schemes. So we were effectively doing his job for him. I knew nothing about Neighbourhood Watch schemes and believed the Superintendent was paid more than enough to do his own work.

A news item rocked the world in the second week of the course. Thomas Harris, a 43-year-old man from Dunblane, drove to Dunblane primary school at 9am on Thursday, 13 March 1996. He parked his van next to a telegraph pole in the school car park and cut the telephone cables. There were seven hundred children in school that day. Including the future tennis stars Andy Murray and his older brother Jamie.

Within five minutes, Harris, wearing shooting earmuffs, had shot and killed sixteen children and a teacher. Fifteen more casualties, mostly children, were injured. Weirdly, using a different gun from the one he had shot and killed the children and teacher with, he put that gun in his mouth and blew the top of his head off. That day, Harris had in his possession seven hundred and forty-three rounds of ammunition and four legally owned handguns - two Browning pistols and two Smith and Wesson Magnum .357 revolvers. (*The most powerful handgun in the world* according to the *Dirty Harry* Films*)*.

Harris was an oddball who may have been incensed that he had been unsuccessful with his application for a position as a volunteer at the school.

The Government addressed the gun law, and handguns that fired rounds above .22 calibre were no longer legal.

The school shootings in America, which occur far too frequently, are a constant reminder of those murdered by Thomas Harris in 1996.

I learned more than most on the course, probably because I had only been a detective for a few months. Roger Crotty brought in DC Alan 'Dog' Rose from the West Midlands Drugs Squad, who presented a real-time drugs arrest and search scenario, parts of which caught everyone out. There is no better way of learning than being made to look stupid in front of twenty-three classmates.

The foundation CID course socially was enjoyable. There was only one rule - what happened on the course stayed on the course. So, I will not mention the Tower Ballroom, Legs Eleven or the Spearmint Rhino - venues I may or may not have visited.

CHAPTER 18

CARRY ON SERGEANT

I attended several post-promotion courses. The new rules regarding disclosure allowed solicitors to have access to statements and information about their client's case before an interview. I was taught how to use CS spray, followed by a diversity course explaining why I should not use CS spray. I also attended courses regarding informant handling and detective tutoring.

My custody sergeant's course at Erdington lasted a week and had a pass/fail exam on the last day. One or two were re-taking the course. I wasn't looking forward to working in the custody block, but the other sergeants on my shift would not have been impressed if I could not take my turn as custody sergeant.

The two instructors were intense and warned that only 70% of students achieved a pass. The lead sergeant pointed to an A4 folder on his desk and said, "This folder includes all the latest stated cases, best practice suggestions, and press articles about cases which collapsed at trial due to the custody sergeant's incompetence."

I arrived early on the second day before the students and instructors. I browsed through the A4 folder out of boredom. Some articles looked complicated, but I found something that piqued my interest. It was a two-page document headed - Custody Sergeants Final Exam 26 April 1996 - this Friday. Twenty questions and detailed answers. I made notes, wiped my fingerprints off the folder and replaced it.

I enjoyed a chat, so the instructors caught me in the crosshairs of their banter. "Dave, do you think Sgt Smith should even bother with the exam on Friday, or shall we reschedule him for another course now?"

Friday at 10am, a sergeant handed out the exam papers. It was the same as the one in the folder. I copied other students with some head scratching and mimicked their perplexed looks. I toyed with getting one question wrong and decided against it. Before announcing the results, both instructors called me into an office. The lead instructor said, "Right, we will not beat about the bush. Can you explain how the hell you got every question right? We have been watching you for a week, and you are neither the brightest nor the hardest working."

"Sorry, gents, and honestly, I had to guess one or two of the answers, but the real credit has to go to the instructors. So well done, you two." They did not believe a word. Police officers can be so suspicious.

An instructor read out the exam results - which included my 100% score. The three sergeants who had failed and were waiting to book another course stared daggers at me.

Peter was diligently working away, preparing for his twelve GCSE exams. Unfortunately, like most sixteen-year-olds, he didn't share his thoughts and fears with his parents. I only got a 'fine' when asked about his revision.

After Peter had finished his exams, I asked how he thought he had done. He said 'okay'.

"Come on son, surely can you tell me a bit more than that?"

"Dad, I have done okay, and that is all you are getting." End of discussion.

England hosted the 1996 European Football Championships. Skinner and Baddiel convinced the country that after thirty years of hurt, "Football was coming home." The nation believed, which was why it was so painful when football didn't come home.

After beating us in the Wembley semi-final, the German fans sang, *It's Coming Home* in English. Ouch.

Gary Lineker, commentating for the BBC, "Football is a game played for ninety minutes, followed by thirty minutes of extra time. Then penalties decide the outcome, and the Germans win. Goodnight." Germany beat Czechoslovakia in the final, and football went home to Munich.

The GCSE exam results that Peter achieved - 5A*'s, 5A's, and 2B's. I don't know what good would have been if that is okay.

He started his A levels, and his head of year noticed Peter had one free period a week and entered him for a GCSE in Psychology.

Peter took that exam a few months later and achieved an A grade. Peter has always felt that he was processed by Solihull School for results.

Peter started work on his A levels, Maths, Further Maths, Physics, English and General studies. I could not see myself being able to help Peter with his homework for any of those subjects.

I started at Rose Road and thought the fifteen-cell custody suite might cause me a problem. I was worried that the instructors from my custody sergeant's course would turn up and spot-check my custody sheets. Then, in a self-righteous tone, "I told you, the thick fucker had cheated, Dave." Dave nodded in agreement and added, "Let's get him back on another course and see how he gets on. 100% my arse."

Luckily for me, Mick Dwyer joined A Unit. He had been an inspector in the Metropolitan Police but transferred to the West Midlands as a constable. Tragically, his wife had died, and with three children, Mick needed to live with his parents in Acocks Green. Mick had transferred as a constable as he was unsure how much commitment he could offer with his domestic situation. Mick was an incredibly talented police officer.

Whenever I struggled in the custody block, I asked the controller to send Mick in. I pointed to the A3 custody sheets and said, "Mick, check them and make me legal." He did. Mick was on A Unit for my time at Rose Road and helped me no end. When Mick sorted out the domestic side of his life, he was promoted and transferred to another force. Thanks again, Mick.

I was the custody sergeant when a detective arrested Pat Roach on suspicion of theft. I was a big fan of *Auf Wiedersehen Pet,* and Pat Roach played 'Bomber'. He was a giant, and apart from being an actor, he was also a wrestler. The arresting officer told me the circumstances and disappeared, leaving us alone in the cell block. Bomber asked, "Sergeant, could I ask you a big favour?"

"You can ask."

"I don't like being in a cell. Could I make tea, sweep the floor, and sit on the bench? Oh, and I will ensure you do not get hurt if it all kicks off."

While none of this was covered in my Custody Sergeants course, I thought it was too good an offer to refuse.

It was nice to hear him speak in his soft Birmingham accent rather than the awful Bristol drawl he used in Auf Wiedersehen Pet. He was delightful company. When a prisoner recognised him, I said that Mr Roach was researching for his part in a movie. Roach was in the custody block for an hour and released without charge. Before he left, he shook my hand, which disappeared into the enormous baseball mitt of his paw. He thanked me and said I was a perfect gent.

After an operation on my back, I returned to work in the intelligence cell. DCI Barry Simpson summoned me. He was unbelievable. He never seemed to go home and loved his job to bits. Barry was always quick to pop the kettle on or 'crash the fags.'

I was in his office while he was on the phone. He was talking to his counterpart from the K division, who asked if he had a couple of officers he could spare for a covert operation. Barry said he did not think so. I tuned in. The job required visiting a lap-dancing club that operated in a school on Thursday evenings. The request by the K Division was to ascertain whether 'any extras' were being offered. I indicated that Mr Simpson should put his hand over the phone and offered the services of DC Paterson and myself.

Bob Paterson and I were dropped off separately at the school with £200 of the K Division's petty cash that Thursday night. We had a gentleman's evening with the local lap dancers. They were not glamour models, more like moms who had popped out to make a few quid before they went to bingo.

I had a private dance and asked the lady what I should do with the swelling in my trousers that she was responsible for. She did not bat an eyelid, "Why don't you take it home and do what you normally do."

We spent all the money and reported that the ladies offered no extras. I suggested that we return the following Thursday just to ensure that no extras were being offered. Mr Simpson told me to clear off.

My Detective Sergeant's course started like most other courses I had attended. Twelve students sat in a circle. An instructor invited us to share a little about ourselves. After five students had churned out some incredibly bland details about their lives and careers, it was the turn of a young, good-looking male sergeant. Those scant details alone rule me out.

"I have twelve years' service." Not dissimilar to the other students so far. "The first person I killed while on duty was someone who stepped onto a zebra crossing in front of my panda car." That was different.

"The second person I killed while on duty was a man who struggled so violently he had a heart attack and died." Even more different.

"The third person I killed while on duty occurred in a large Wolverhampton shopping centre. I was with a colleague, and we detained a shoplifter. He threw us around like a pair of rag dolls and tried to strangle us. We were eventually able to overpower and restrain him but had to wait so long for backup he died of asphyxia."

That made Neil, by definition, a fully qualified serial killer. He eventually became a senior police officer, so I assume he focused on his police career and stopped murdering members of the public.

Peter took a Saturday job at Gordon Scott's shoe shop on the High Street in Solihull. He worked in the children's section from 9am to 6pm. *Toy Story* was played on a video loop to distract and entertain the kids. Peter still struggles to watch that film without twitching.

Peter applied for a pilot scholarship with the RAF, which would financially support him through his A Levels.

He hadn't heard anything for over a month, so I phoned the admin department at RAF Cranwell. I asked how many pilot scholarship applications the RAF had received. When I was told 100,000 applicants had applied for one hundred scholarships, I felt deflated and said,

"Christ, my son has got no chance, then." The very polite lady asked,

"Is your son very clever?"

"Yes, he is."

I never forgot what she said next, "Well, why would we not award him a scholarship? I don't even know your son, but I have more confidence in him than you do. The results will be out in the next couple of weeks. Thank you for calling."

Peter was awarded the scholarship and committed to a career as a pilot in the RAF. I was so proud.

I applied to be a Detective Sergeant. I was successful and offered a position at Kings Heath police station. I turned down that offer. I enjoyed being at Rose Road. The management team of Chief Superintendent John Scott, Detective Superintendent Barry Simpson, Chief Inspector Angie James and Detective Inspector Chris Pretty were incredibly talented and, more importantly, they cared about their staff. I decided to wait until a position in the Rose Road office became available. I remained in the Intelligence Cell.

In 1997, under Tony Blair, the Labour Party won the most significant landslide victory in general election history. Blair became England's youngest Prime Minister since 1812. John Major left office reflecting on his time as Prime Minister while possibly trying to forget the more lurid details of his affair with Edwina Currie.

In June 1998, Dave Collins was promoted to Inspector and moved on. I took his place as a Detective Sergeant in the main office.

CHAPTER 19

THE CID OFFICE

The CID office accommodated four teams, each led by a detective sergeant. Nominally, the teams covered an area. Each team had four detectives/temporary detectives. Each DS reported to DI Chris Pretty - The Captain. His office was opposite the main CID office, and he ensured our behaviour did not become too raucous.

In my first week, Mr Pretty posted me to a couple of split duties. An early start - off duty at 1pm, then a return to work at 5pm to cover lates. These were inconvenient and unpopular, but as the new bloke, I knew it was only a test. Being on the CID with my own team was what I had worked for.

Arriving for work early, I saw that the CID had three prisoner packages. One was for someone I had previously dealt with. While reading that package, Mr Pretty arrived, and I thought I might have scored brownie points for being keen. Wrong. I learned extremely quickly that Mr Pretty was in charge. "Sergeant Smith, you will not deal with the package you are reading. Here is yours. Give that one to Sergeant Bebbington when he arrives."

I submitted my pocketbook, overtime, and expenses at the end of each month. My basic wage packet would receive a much-appreciated top-up if my submissions were in order.

A Detective Sergeants meeting took place at 10am on the first Monday of the month. The Captain dealt with internal issues and housekeeping. DI Pretty spoke to two of his trusted lieutenants an hour before, and they gave him a heads-up, so he was not blindsided at the meeting. I was never one of the Captain's lieutenants. I don't know why. It wasn't as if I would ever write a book or anything.

Mr Pretty demanded loyalty, and his message was clear - if you were unhappy working for him, find an alternative and leave. The quality of his briefings was straight out of an Army training manual. His instructions and advice were clear and precise, and his audience listened while making notes in their blue notebooks.

Apart from the Temporary Detectives, everyone else was there because DI Pretty wanted them. TDCs worked two three-month stints with two Detective Sergeants. Other arrivals to the Rose Road CID happened when someone from another area had a problem and would likely lose their detective status. If DI Pretty or DCI Simpson rated them, they were thrown a lifeline and worked as detectives at Rose Road.

The most experienced sergeant in the office was Andy Bebbington. He hailed from the Black Country, had a dodgy perm and was a fitness fanatic. He called everyone 'Old Pal' and used expressions that I never understood, one of which was, "I've done more overtime this month than you can shake a shitty stick at, Old Pal."

Andy told me that his Superintendent once wrote on his appraisal, "Sergeant Bebbington is destined to become either one of the best detectives this police force has ever seen or a problem prisoner in HMP Birmingham."

I liked Andy. He worked hard, and I am sure the vast amount of overtime he incurred was purely coincidental.

Moira Foulger was a temporary detective in the office. We had worked together on A Unit at Rose Road. She was black-haired, voluptuous and softly spoken. She was bubbly but nervous. Some people thought that made her weak. Some people were wrong. Ireland was her spiritual home, even if she was probably born in Moseley, Birmingham.

One of her cases involved a vulnerable woman from Liverpool who had fallen in love with a violent criminal from Birmingham. The young lady was wined and dined for two days and shown around the sights of Brum. On the third day, her life changed. She was delivered to a seedy massage parlour and instructed to entertain five punters an hour. She was controlled by a violent man in a City a hundred miles from her home.

After a few weeks, she escaped and fled to her parents. Emotionally, they supported her, and her GP treated the traumatised young woman. Her family managed to coax from her the details of her horrific experience. They reported this matter to the police, and the DCI allocated the enquiry to TDC Foulger.

Moira took a detailed statement from the victim. The advice and guidance she received from colleagues and some senior officers suggested this case would never get to court. They advised Moira to inform the victim that a Crown Court trial would cause her more distress and pain. Moira ignored the advice, traced the suspect and arrested him. During his interview, the suspect ridiculed the victim and her complaint. He was charged and opted for trial at Crown Court.

Moira spent hours with the victim and helped her prepare for the ordeal of giving evidence. At the trial, the jury listened to her harrowing evidence. They also heard the glib and dismissive account of the defendant.

The jury deliberated for an hour and convicted the defendant of 'Living off Immoral Earnings'. I bumped into Moira at Crown Court while the defendant was waiting to be sentenced. She was so proud of herself and said, "Sarge, I knew I was doing the right thing. Everybody who gave me advice had never even met the victim. She needed lots of help and support, and I knew I could do that."

The defendant was sentenced to five-years in prison.

Moira didn't stop there. She saw a man who had been sexually abused while he was a child at a children's home in Birmingham. Moira took a forty-page statement detailing his systematic ill-treatment. The details were harrowing and compelling.

As Moira had left it on her desk, I read part of the statement. Moira had beautiful handwriting, and her attention to detail was impressive. An extract from the statement still resonates. The victim recalled that when the lady at the children's home put him to bed, he always asked, "Miss, can you tuck me in really tight, please?" He explained to Moira that this would sometimes prevent the paedophile, who worked nights, from getting his hand down his bed sheets. Sadly, it did not always work.

The victim named offenders and other victims. The DCI expected a few bland pages over which he could deliberate and decide that a single complaint did not warrant further investigation. As a result of Moira's actions, a HOLMES enquiry into abuse at several children's homes in Birmingham was launched. The incident room traced dozens of offenders and victims, and the enquiry cost millions of pounds. The DCI removed Moira from the investigation.

Over a coffee, I asked Moira how she made sure her enquiries made it to court. "Sarge, if I see a victim and get their account. Supervision will give me a list of instructions about how to achieve what the organisation wanted - which was usually no further action. However, if I take a forty-page statement with loads of detail, there is not a lot they can do. Not many senior officers are brave enough to chuck a victim's statement into the bin. Even if they did, I kept copies."

Things worked out for Moira.

Peter was prepping for his A Levels. Of course, I cared but knew better than to intrude. His nominated University was Manchester. Based on his academic achievements at Solihull School, Peter should have been a 'Bencher' - A sixth-form prefect with benefits that included a flashy blazer.

I met the headmaster, Mr Lee, to speak about this matter. He said that because Peter had not applied for

Oxford or Cambridge, he had not been awarded Bencher status. Mr Lee confirmed that twenty-two six-form students had applied for Oxbridge. I asked isn't that enough?

"To be honest, Mr Smith, twenty-three would have been nice. Good day."

Peter achieved four A's and a B at GCSE A Level, which I thought was brilliant, though he felt it was okay.

Over the following months, Mark Ellis, Shane Saunders, Andy Bentley and Russ McCall worked on my team. They had all been panda drivers at Rose Road and knew the area and the criminals. They worked hard and breezed through the TDC process.

One guy joined my team, and though he tried, CID work didn't suit him. He requested a return to uniform duties - a brave decision as he could easily have stayed and just coasted. He was promoted to sergeant a few years later, so well done, Nathan.

CHAPTER 20

IT'S STILL NOT COMING HOME

In May 1998, England set off to France to compete in the Football World Cup. With a blend of youth, experience and Glen Hoddle as manager, the expectation was tangible. England drew Tunisia, Romania and Columbia, not exactly a 'Group of Death.' It might just happen this time.

Most will remember England's first game against Tunisia for all the wrong reasons. Following years of domestic abuse, the Tunisian supporters were ready to resolve their grievances against the establishment.

They encountered English fans with a propensity for violence tanked up and ripened by the sun. Bottle-throwing and flag burning resulted in the French police formally introducing themselves with repeated baton charges and hundreds of arrests. The UK charts, not for the first time, had read the room correctly, Karl Douglas reclaiming the number one spot with *Kung Fu Fighting.*

England won two matches and lost one, which resulted in a knock-out game against the old enemy Argentina. Roared on by the English fans and with Fat Les in the UK charts with *Vindaloo,* what could go wrong?

In a nutshell, David Beckham was sent off shortly after half-time. An over-fussy referee disallowed a Sol Campbell goal, and we lost in a penalty shoot-out.

The 2002 World Cup will take place in Korea, hopefully too far away and too expensive a journey for our knuckle-dragging supporters to attend.

Peter accepted Manchester University's offer of a three-year Mechanical Engineering degree course. He received financial assistance from the RAF and became an Officer Cadet at the Universities Air Squadron.

When Peter left home, I was so upset I didn't eat for weeks. My stomach just knotted and churned. I knew that Pete would be okay. I was worried about myself. When *Toy Story 3* was released, knowing it revolved around Andy leaving home. I couldn't watch it and still haven't.

On a Saturday at 11pm in Winson Green, the police received reports that members of the public had heard gunshots.

The following morning, I arrived for work at 8am; the night note and package were handed to me when I came on duty. The night detective had been unable to trace the intended victim or his attacker. The City hospital confirmed they had not admitted anyone with gunshot injuries in the previous twelve hours.

With four of my team and a uniformed officer, I set off to Winson Green to conduct an area search followed by house-to-house enquiries. At the scene, I briefed the officers. We attracted some attention from the locals, but that didn't matter. It may even encourage someone to come forward, and as it happened, it did.

I stood beside a black VW Golf near which the night detective had recovered three spent 9 mm bullet casings. I opened with, "Ladies and gents. Last night, a man, possibly in his early twenties, was standing here when two men confronted him. One was holding a handgun and started shooting at him. The intended victim ran away."

A member of the public in his early twenties challenged me,

"No, he didn't." I asked,

"How do you know that?"

"Because it was me they were fucking shooting at."

If that was true, this young man was far more qualified to conduct the briefing than me, so I invited him to continue.

"I was there." He pointed at a lamppost. "I saw two blokes. One fired three rounds at me, and his gun jammed. I didn't hang around to find out whether he could fix his gun. I don't know who they are, but I will make my own fucking enquiries." I asked,

"What happened next?"

"Let me show you, officer." He sprinted off and did not come back.

I made some notes to correct the information on the crime report. Though we had a much clearer picture of what happened, evidentially, it did not help the investigation.

I was dealing with an assault by a prison officer on an inmate at HMP Birmingham. The circumstances were that the prison officer entered a cell to threaten an inmate as he had been slagging him off on C

Wing. The prison officer offered to fight the inmate in the showers. The inmate declined, and the prison officer tried to head-butt him, missed and gashed his head on a locker. The injured officer sounded his whistle, and the other prison officers who attended wrongly assumed their colleague had been assaulted.

The inmate sustained substantial injuries while being removed from his cell and taken to the hospital wing. Every prisoner on the landing said they had seen the prison officer attacking the inmate.

Andy Bebbington was surprised that two prison officers had made statements incriminating their colleague. There were only two or three detectives in the CID office, and Andy looked at me as he slowly walked the length of the room to where I sat. In hushed tones, he asked, "Old pal, do you know how three Hells Angels keep a secret?" I had no idea and said so. "One of them kills the other two." Having shared this pearl of wisdom, he strolled back to his desk.

Moira and I interviewed the prison officer under caution at Rose Road. He had a solicitor and a Prison Officers Association representative. I gave the solicitor full disclosure, and he had a conference with his client.

An hour later, we all sat in an interview room. The solicitor took a chair and sat as far away from his client as possible. At the start of the interview, those present introduced themselves. I asked the solicitor if he wanted to say anything before the interview started. "Yes, I most certainly would. I have given legal advice to this prison officer. He has decided to ignore that advice. Whatever he chooses to say has nothing to do with me. Well, that was different.

I cautioned the prison officer and explained that he did not have to say anything unless he wanted to. I confirmed the incident date, time and place and invited the prison officer to give his account. "Right, that fucker had been slagging me off for weeks on C Wing. I was not having that. I went to his cell and told his cellmate to leave." The solicitor sat in the corner, shaking his head. The POA rep shrugged, and the prison officer continued. "I invited the prisoner to join me in the showers."
I asked, "Was that so he could shower and maybe calm the situation down?"

"No, we were going there to sort things out, man to man."

"A fight?"

"Abso-fucking-lutely, the little shit wouldn't come out of his cell. We had a scuffle, and I tried to head-butt him, missed and gashed my head on a locker." His solicitor was already packing away his papers. As soon as I switched off the interview tape, he stood up, shook his head, and glared at his client. He politely said, "Thank you, officers," and left the room.

I accompanied Moira to HMP Birmingham. We were there to check the layout of C Wing and ascertain what the inmates could physically see from their cells. Moira wore a pretty red frock. When the inmates of C Wing saw Moira, they burst into an appalling but well-intended rendition of the Chris De Berg classic *'Lady in Red'*.

Most prisoners said they had seen the unprovoked attack on the inmate from their cells, which was impossible. Most prison officers had seen nothing. We took dozens of statements, and I prepared a file for a CPS decision.

Senior Crown Prosecutor Bob Lambden deliberated for a month. His written response concluded that he could not find a truthful thread on which the CPS could put a case before the courts. He added that the Governor of HMP Birmingham should have a serious conversation with the prison officer who instigated the incident to establish, "Exactly which medieval institution does he think he works in?"

In July 1999, Wayne Jones joined my team. He had passed the sergeant's exam and was an excellent investigator. Mr Pretty invited us into his office for a briefing. Wayne and I had our blue books open and our pens poised.

An ambulance crew had attended a flat in Ladywood and found a lifeless three-year-old boy. The child's mother was separated from the father and lived with her son and lesbian girlfriend. The mother had gone out overnight.

In the morning, the girlfriend found the child lifeless on his bed and put him in a bath to revive him. When that didn't work, she called an ambulance, which arrived at 1pm. By this time, the mother had returned home and travelled with her son to the hospital. Attempts to revive the child at the scene, en route to and at the hospital, were unsuccessful, and the little boy was pronounced dead.

The woman looking after the child refused to speak about her relationship with the boy and denied assaulting him. Without a witness or evidence of an assault, we were hopeful the pathologist's report would explain the cause of death.

Wayne and I went to see the little boy's grandparents. They were devastated, and their grief was raw. They kept asking, "Why didn't she leave him with us? We loved having him. He was never any trouble."

Two further post-mortems were conducted, which Mr Pretty attended and spared me the ordeal. For that, I will be forever grateful. Mr Pretty said there was almost nothing of the young lad left after the third post-mortem. The little boy had been fit and healthy, and there was no medical explanation for a natural cause of death. Four fingertip-sized bruises on his sternum were his only injury. They indicated that he had possibly been assaulted.

The grandparents invited Wayne and me to the funeral. We attended the church service, and a horse-drawn carriage carried the tiny coffin. The funeral was heartbreaking.

Wayne and I interviewed the suspect, but she decided not to comment. The child's mother stated that she had been away at a party and had not returned until after her son had died, which was confirmed.

Wayne and I liaised with the CPS and a paediatric medical expert. The paediatrician stated that a single blow to the stomach was the most likely cause of death. CPS had several questions about the family set-up, and it was time to resolve them.

Wayne and I spoke to the mother at Rose Road, and I asked if she would provide a family background statement. Her response stunned me. "Unless my girlfriend is found guilty, I will not make a statement."

Well, her comment implied a lot, but evidentially, it meant nothing. I thought she wanted answers as long as they were the ones she wanted to hear. Reliant on the circumstantial evidence and the paediatrician's statement, the CPS authorised a charge of manslaughter.

My father was dying of lung cancer in Redditch Hospital and had only hours to live. I waited outside the Hospital with Hughie, Anthony and Peter for confirmation that he had passed.

My mother launched into her final act of vindictiveness. Fearing the family might rally around my Dad, she booked herself into a hospice. Given that she lived for ten more years, I think she had another agenda. My Dad was sixty-nine when he died.

I went back to work the day after my Dad died. Chief Superintendent John Scott saw me in the station car park. He told me he had heard about my Dad and offered his condolences.

"Vince, I know you think you can deal with anything, and you have a lot of work on. But this will hit you hard. You are now on compassionate leave, and I will see you in a fortnight. If there is anything I can do, let me know. Now go home."

Mr Scott was an absolute gentleman whose support I appreciated.

As the manslaughter trial approached, the paediatrician, the only prosecution witness, became increasingly concerned. He kept changing his statement, not the detailed content, only the grammar.

At the trial, the reason became apparent. The defence had secured an expert who had not only tutored our witness at university but also did not regard him as professionally competent. While our witness gave evidence, the defence expert sat shaking his head. He reduced the key prosecuting witness into a mumbling, bumbling wreck. As he left the court, he continued to make written amendments to his statement. Coleman Treacy QC, the prosecuting barrister, shouted, "It's a bit fucking late now."

When the trial reached half-time, the defence submitted that there was no case to answer. After a short deliberation, the Judge agreed. I had hoped that the Crown Court trial would provide answers for the grandparents. Sadly, it hadn't. Throughout that investigation, Wayne Jones had been exceptional. Rest in Peace, K.

Shortly after 8am one Friday morning, the Chief Superintendent who had replaced John Scott charged into the CID office and confronted me, "Sergeant Smith, your team are not putting enough doors in. Get out there and rattle some cages."

I would have liked to have had a battle of wits with him, but I don't fight with unarmed men.

The same morning, my team set off to Acocks Green to arrest a man suspected of burglary. I took the entire team. A few years before, the suspect had called the police to hand himself in as he knew a warrant was outstanding for his arrest. The officers who attended opened the back door of the panda car and invited him to join them. The 'prisoner' violently attacked both officers.

I briefed my troops. Shane and Russ went around the back, and I was at the front with Dave Harbon and Mark Ellis. I knocked on the front door. It was a loud knock, the sort of knock that indicated that the police had arrived on official business and would not be leaving until that business had been concluded. There was no answer.

I knocked on the door again, no answer. Then I heard an almighty crash. We ran to the back of the house. Russ and Shane stood on the shattered remains of a pair of double-glazed patio doors. Russ held a house brick and said, "Sarge, I thought I could smell gas. You can't be too careful these days."

Shane chipped in, "If that knob complains that we haven't put enough doors in, point out these two that we did today, sarge."

There was no arrest, but a point well made.

In July 2000, I entered a ballot at my local David Lloyds Tennis Club. I won tickets for the men's singles final at Wimbledon.

On the 9 July, I saw Pete Sampras beat Patrick Rafter in four sets to win his seventh and final Wimbledon. After his victory, Sampras shared the moment by joining his parents in the crowd.

After the final, I was still buzzing and decided to have a curry and a beer to wind down. I knew this day had been a once-in-my-lifetime experience.

I sat in an empty curry house and ordered a beer and a lamb Madras with all the trimmings. I had a few sips of lager, and then a customer walked in. He approached my table and asked, "Excuse me, mate, would you mind if I joined you?"

I wasn't particularly looking for company, so I paused. The guy explained, "I'm a long-distance lorry driver and spend most of my time alone. I have been on the road since early this morning, and honestly, I wouldn't mind a meal and having a chat."

He seemed genuine enough, and I didn't want to appear rude.so I said, "No problem, sit down and have a beer," I called a waiter over and ordered my guest a lager. He seemed like a nice guy, and we chatted. Sadly, he had no interest in tennis and no idea that the Wimbledon men's singles final had even taken place. He wasn't happy about the state of the motorway network around London. I knew as much about motorways as he did about Pete Sampras's incredible first serve. We moved on, and he asked what I did for a living. I told him that I was a policeman in Birmingham. My impromptu dinner guest said, "I don't really know Birmingham."

"Never mind." I dipped my nan bread into my curry and resigned myself to having a nice meal, with a side dish of drivel.

"In fact, I only know one person in Birmingham. Mind you, he's a copper."

We were two men in London, a copper from Birmingham and a lorry driver from somewhere up north. What were the chances?

"He is called Hughie McGowan. Does that name mean anything to you?" I looked at him, then scanned the room for video cameras. Maybe Jeremy Beadle was punting out another series about winding up innocent members of the public. The lorry driver knew Hughie from the Lamp Tavern pub in Digbeth. I still find it hard to believe.

Kevin Hyland started working on the CID at Rose Road. He had served in the Met and Northampton police forces. Kevin was not very tall, and as his hair was brushed back, he was nicknamed Sonic. He was as industrious as the magic ring collecting Sonic the Hedgehog on the mega drive game system. The only thing Kevin did not have was a pause button.

The F2 had a spate of robberies at the Winson Green post office. Elderly women were robbed of their pensions and pushed to the ground by their attacker. Their descriptions of their attacker were useless. The age of the victims and the physical pain they suffered meant their statements were a record of the incidents rather than crucial evidence. There were very few lines of enquiry.

I was with Kevin, and we were leaving Birmingham Magistrates Court. Over the radio, we heard that a panda car had stopped a man acting suspiciously near the Winson Green post office. Officers were in the process of checking him out. Sonic set off at a rate of knots. We were with the officers in seconds. Sonic did not even have time to collect any magic rings en route. We thanked the officers and said we would take it from there.

The man said he was uncomfortable talking to the police in public and invited us to join him in his flat.

He pointed to his flat on the third floor of a tower block that directly overlooked the post office.

As we walked into his flat, there was a saucer on a coffee table and a small rock of crack cocaine on that saucer. Well, that was a game-changer. Kevin arrested the man for possession of a class-A drug and cautioned him. Kevin shook his head, pointed at the piece of crack and said, "It's not your fault." The suspect said,

"I honestly didn't mean to hurt them. I just needed the money."

I arrested the man on suspicion of committing a series of robberies. We took him to the custody suite at Rose Road. The custody sergeant asked if he wished to have legal representation for his interviews, which he declined.

He made a full and frank admission to six robberies. He stated he saw his victims enter the post office and robbed the women as they walked out. He returned to his flat, kept the cash, and disposed of their purse or handbag down the block's rubbish chute. He apologised for the offences and said he needed the money to buy drugs. He pleaded guilty at Birmingham Crown Court and received a six-year prison sentence.

My area included HMP Birmingham. Mr Pretty called me into his office. A prisoner named Smith, using a shoelace as a ligature, had committed suicide in his cell.

The prison system allowed prisons to 'exchange' problem prisoners. HMP Birmingham had a prisoner who the prison population believed to be a police informant, and his life was in danger. Smith was a persistent suicide risk. The prisons agreed to swap prisoners, and Smith found himself in HMP Birmingham.

HMP Blakenhurst records confirmed that staff had confiscated dozens of Smith's ligatures during his time there. He threatened to kill himself daily, and when asked to hand over his ligatures, he did.

Smith arrived at HMP Birmingham at 3.55pm and died shortly before 5pm - he survived four months at Blakenhurst and just over an hour in Winson Green. The only outcome from the inquiry was my belief that a cup of tea or a kind word could have prevented his death.

In April 2000, Kevin Hyland joined me for a coffee in the canteen. He told me he was planning a three-day police operation in Winson Green. He was confident it would be successful, but only if he had my team's total commitment.

His operation started on the following Tuesday. Monday was our leave day, and my team came in and cleared our desks. Sorting out property reminders, CPS memos, ID parades and police bail issues.

Tuesday morning, we all reported to Kevin, who kept us busy. Kevin placed police portacabins around the area. He had uniform officers and detectives proactively patrolling the crime hotspots he had identified. Dozens of uniformed officers patrolled the area to reassure the public. Kevin dug out arrest warrants that had been outstanding for months.

The master stroke he pulled involved the houses that had operated as drug dens for years. It was usually early morning when police officers executed drugs warrants. The occupants had devoured whatever drugs had been available, and the police left without evidence or prisoners.

Kevin did it differently. Raids took place even earlier. Officers recovered evidence of drug-taking activity - syringes, burnt silver foil, bongs and ashtrays. The police charged the tenant with 'permitting their premises to be used to supply drugs'. Birmingham City Council served a notice on the prisoner, terminating their tenancy agreement. The Council sealed the windows and doors of the address. The arrested person was now of 'no fixed abode' and remanded in custody. Kevin knew what he was doing and how to do it.

Officers on the operation made dozens of arrests and recovered stolen property. For three days, Winson Green was a crime-free area.

I don't know where Kevin Hyland moved to, but he will make a difference.

In 2001, Peter achieved his degree in Mechanical Engineering and was awarded a Desmond Tutu (2:2). I am reliably informed (by Peter's lovely wife, Jude) that his decent grade resulted from a mercurial effort in the last few months of his course.

Well done, Pete. Your next mission, if you choose to accept, is a career as a fast jet pilot in the RAF.

On 26 June 2003, I started work on an enquiry after a young black man, Esron Germaine, had been shot at point-blank range and hospitalised. He was not expected to survive and never regained consciousness. According to the pathologist, a ball bearing fired from a ball bearing gun ricocheted off almost every major organ in Esron's body.

Initial enquiries revealed the deceased had a connection with Birmingham's Burger Bar gang. His friends were evasive. Three females who were near the scene when the police arrived made statements denying any knowledge of the murder or the victim.

The SIO was Andy Hough. He often had a workload of more than ten murder cases in his briefcase. DCI Hough, supported by CCTV and telephone data, charged the three females with conspiring to pervert the course of justice. The evidence against them was that they had denied owning mobile phones. When the police traced their mobile phone numbers, their call data revealed they were all at the scene of the murder. The traffic from their phones incriminated two male friends of Esron. Though circumstantial, it suggested that they were all involved in Esron's death.

Intelligence indicated that the week before his shooting, Esron had been to Swindon. Andy Hough sent me to Swindon with five detectives to conduct house-to-house enquiries.

I visited Swindon police station and spoke to a Chief Inspector who said the beat officer who covered the area we were interested in was PC Justin Davies. He added that Justin was extremely hardworking and had produced dozens of surveillance logs for the address we were interested in.

I partnered up with DC Dave Baker, who had worked on the MIU for some time. I intended to complete this line of inquiry in a day. One pub had to be visited, and Dave Baker suggested we had a pint before we returned to Brum.

Dave and I conducted house-to-house enquiries at a row of bungalows occupied by pensioners. At the last address, we met a nervous couple who were initially concerned. When I said I knew PC Justin Davies, the lady of the house said, "Oh if he knows Justin, we can tell him everything."

They explained that the police had put a camera in their front window, which overlooked a 'house of interest', and the camera linked to their video recorder. I said, "I suppose the police collected the videos from you." The lady said, "No, we had to view the video and write logs of what was on the bloody thing. One time, we almost missed an episode of Frost because Justin needed the written logs for a Monday morning briefing."

The police retrieved the surveillance camera, and the target of their operation was now deceased. These two lovely people could stand down and never miss an episode of Frost. I do not think Justin Davies was as hardworking as his Chief Inspector thought.

At 6pm, Dave and I walked into 'The Deer's Leap' public house. I saw a Deer's head in a glass case above a roaring log fire. The bar looked like the headquarters for 'Combat 18'. Shaved heads, St George's Cross flags, Swastika tattoos and Pitbull terriers tied to tattooed wrists. We ordered a pint while the locals had a case conference. The oldest and ugliest of the group walked over to speak to us. "What do you two pricks want?" In the circumstances, this felt like quite a gentle introduction.

"We are from the CID in Birmingham and are here on a murder enquiry…"

The tattooed fuckwit interrupted, "Whoa, you really are fucking boring me now. What do you want?"

"Okay, I have a picture of a youth, and we know he was in this area the week before he was murdered. I want to know if you have seen him in this pub. If we get an answer, we will be on our way."

"Okay, show me the photo.' I handed him the picture of a teenage black male.

The skinhead smiled and asked, "What's his name?"

"Esron."

Without looking up, he said, "What's the name of this pub?"

"The Deer's Leap, why?"

The skinhead said, "If that fucker had come in here, then this pub would have been renamed 'Esron's Leap,' and young Esron would have been put in that glass cabinet, replacing the fucking deer's head."

I took this to mean that Esron had not visited this establishment.

At the murder trial, the two 'friends' of the deceased were represented by the well-prepared Pat Thomas QC. Mr Redgrave QC was a last-minute prosecuting counsel replacement. Mr Thomas was able to discredit the prosecution's three female witnesses. Even though they made incredibly detailed statements, fully explaining the events that led to the shooting of Esron Germaine. - It started with a row between friends, but as Esron was bigger and stronger than the other two, to overpower Esron, they had to shoot him.

However, as the police had charged the women with perverting the course of justice, Mr Thomas pointed out repeatedly that if the police believed they had lied, a jury could not possibly rely on their evidence in a murder trial. Mr Thomas also pointed out that the incident room had only focused on the suspects. He added theatrically that the incident room was "Without doubt, a room with a very blinkered view."

Mr Thomas only needed to show there was an element of doubt. Which he did. The defendants were acquitted. Sadly, none of Esron's family turned up at the trial. The only people interested in the outcome were DC Dave Harbon and me.

In July 2003, I was not busy enough, so I decided to make my life a little more interesting with two life-changing adjustments. Firstly, as I was now divorced for the second time, Sarah and I decided to get married. I booked the Moon Palace in Cancun, Mexico, for the wedding and an all-inclusive two-week honeymoon. Peter brought his girlfriend, Jude. Six-year-old Marcus and Josef made up our wedding party. The location was picture perfect.

The Mexican marriage procedure was different. Sarah and I had to have a blood sample taken four days before the wedding. The ever-inquisitive Josef tagged along. The nurse had a moustache of Emiliano Zapata proportions and the voice of a one-hundred cigarettes-a-day chain smoker. I resigned myself to comply with whatever she requested. She growled, "Arm."

I rolled up my shirtsleeve and presented my left arm. The nurse plunged a hypodermic syringe into my vein with the same amount of force as a lifesaving adrenalin shot. I held back the tears as she drew blood.

The angelic Josef had a question and, as ever, would not be denied. "Excuse me. Can I ask why you take blood samples from people getting married?" That was an excellent question, one that perhaps Sarah or I should have asked. The nurse used Josef's query to take a smoke break, opened a pack of cigarettes and lit up. She stared at Josef, and took a harsh drag on her fag, then growled, "It's for the Syphilis and the Aids."

It was not like Josef did not have enough questions to ask on any normal day. So, thank you to the chain-smoking nurse with the droopy moustache.

Apparently, if the blood samples tested positive for either Syphilis or Aids, the marriage is not considered legal.

The month after our wedding, Tommy, our son, was born. Well, that should keep me busy for the next few years.

David Crigman QC, a talented barrister who regularly shredded police officers during his cross-examination, was in Michelle's, a wine bar on Corporation Street. That wine bar was a watering hole for the legal fraternity. Senior police officers were welcome, while the rank and file, like me, were tolerated.

I was with Stephen Linehan QC, who had verbally battered me over an issue regarding the forthcoming trial of a corrupt police officer he was prosecuting, and I was the OIC. Mr Linehan said, "Sergeant Smith, your inability to do your job is making it nigh on impossible for me to fucking do mine."

After the bell had rang for the end of that round, Mr Linehan told me it was my round and pointed to the bar. I ordered a large glass of wine and pointed to Mr Linehan. The barman was more than aware of Mr Linehan's preferred tipple and filled a wine glass.

Mr Linehan was now involved in a much friendlier exchange with Mr Crigman. I stood there like a prize plum holding Mr Linehan's glass of wine. He took the glass, had a sip and said, "David, I don't know if you have ever met him, but this is Detective Sergeant Smith."

Mr Crigman cast his barristers beady over me, shook my hand and said, "No, Stephen, I don't think Sergeant Smith and I have ever crossed swords in a Crown Court exchange."

That was true - we hadn't. It would have been a mismatch. Crigman would have brandished a sword of Aragorn from *Lord of the Rings* proportions, whereas I would have had to defend myself with a butter knife.

I watched the banter between the QCs, which was legal high-brow stuff. I smiled and nodded. Mr Crigman finished his drink and declined Mr Linehan's generous offer of my paying for a refill. Mr Crigman turned to me, "Sergeant Smith, can I give you some advice?"

"Of course, sir."

"If you ever find yourself in the witness box and, as the defence barrister, I am about to start your cross-examination, remember these words. *Do not even attempt to answer any of my first five questions.*"

I was puzzled, "Why is that Mr Crigman?"

"Sergeant, I would not have asked you any of those questions if you could answer them."

Mr Crigman left. I was confused.

Mr Linehan explained that it was a trap. Police officers always believed they knew everything about their investigation. As the prosecution's case is presented first, a police officer will have been tossed gentle volleys and lobs by the prosecuting barrister, which the officer will have swatted away with a smug smile.

Having found obscure issues within the thousands of documents generated in a case, the defence barrister cross-examines the officer. Who, having failed to answer the first three or four questions, becomes anxious and is tempted to guess an answer. In a Crown Court trial, that was a fatal mistake and naturally opened the door to - "Officer, my client could be imprisoned for the rest of his life. Have you attended court to give evidence, or are you going to guess the answers to all of my questions?"

Thank you for the lesson, Gents.

Working on Incident Rooms meant I would meet and chat with staff engaged with other enquiries. One guy, Mick, a detective from the K Division, usually had a tale to tell, and we swapped stories. I hadn't seen him for a couple of months, so when I did, we had some catching up to do. He opened, "I've got one for you, Wolfie. You'll love this."

Mick looked through a folder and selected a police command and control log. I thought, wow, he needs props for this story. It must be good. "Wolfie, I need to explain the background first. I was on duty and sent to an address because a neighbour had heard god-awful screams and thought someone was being murdered."

He paused, had a drink of coffee and continued, "It was a ground-floor flat, and a guy wearing a blood-stained dressing gown answered the front door. He told me his name was Paul, and he lived in the flat with his partner, Eric, and their Pit Bull Terrier, Spike. I could hear sobs and muffled screams coming from the lounge, so I walked past Paul to check it out. Eric was naked on a settee and screaming into the cushion he held with his left hand. His right hand clutched his groin in a futile attempt to stem the fountain of blood spraying the lounge. Spike was sat innocently, almost whistling, in a corner of the lounge."

Mick paused. I sipped my black coffee, and then he continued. "I asked Paul, What the fuck has happened here, chap? Paul took a deep breath and said I suppose you're going to find out anyway… we were playing sex games when Eric decided to involve Spike, who wasn't too keen. It was Eric's bright idea to get a jar of Marmite out of the kitchen and smear the contents onto his cock and bollocks."

We both had a drink of coffee. Mick continued, "While Eric was thinking naughty, kinky sex games, Spike thought his dinner, meat with two veg, had been served and tucked in. The Pit Bull has only bitten off and eaten Eric's cock and balls." I was riveted, Mick continued.

"The controller confirmed the ambulance was only minutes away. I gave him my update, which he wrote on the log, and here it is." He produced the Command-and-Control log -
Update from the officer at the scene - I am in a flat with two men and their Pit Bull Terrier. There are no other parties involved. The Pit Bull Terrier attacked one of the men, who sustained horrific injuries. At this time, I can confirm that the victim's genitals are outstanding. Mick said, "I put that bit in about the outstanding genitals, brilliant eh."

I thought if anyone described my genitals as outstanding, I would prefer to be still attached to them.

"Christ, Mick, that sounds horrendous. How do you get over something like that?"
Mick finished his coffee, lit a cigarette and solemnly said, "Wolfie, you're right, and honestly, this has had quite an effect on me."

"In what way?" Mick paused,

"You know, I used to love a bit of Marmite on my toast in the morning, but since this incident, I have marmalade."

I giggled at that, then asked, "Anyway, Mick, how is Eric doing?"

"Sadly, Eric is no longer with us." I was shocked.

"Bloody hell, that is terrible. What an awful way to go."
Mick took a drag on his cigarette and poured himself another coffee. He continued.

"Yep, Eric is gone, but do you want the good news?"

"Good news, Mick, really. Is there any good news?"

"Yep, the doctors have said that in the fullness of time, <u>Erica</u> should make a full recovery."

Mick and I lost it in an uncontrollable fit of giggles.

CHAPTER 21

FINAL DISCLOSURE

Murder trials in America are different and often more theatrical than in this country. I read about the trial of a man charged with the murder of his wife. Though the police never found the woman's body, there was plenty of circumstantial evidence against her husband.

As the trial approached its conclusion, the defence attorney made a plea directly to the jury, "Ladies and Gentlemen, could you all please look at the clock in the courtroom." He pointed to the clock. "The time is three minutes to one o'clock. At exactly 1pm, the woman referred to by the prosecution throughout this trial as 'the deceased' will walk through that door." He pointed to the door to the courtroom. "When that happens, the judge will discharge the case against my client, and he will go home a free man."

In complete silence, the court waited. The clock dramatically struck 1pm. The door hadn't opened. The defence attorney made his final plea to the jury. "Ladies and gentlemen, the fact that you were watching that door indicates that there must be some doubt in your minds that anyone has been murdered. If that is the case, you must return a verdict of not guilty and acquit my client."

The jury retired and, within an hour, delivered their verdict. To the single charge of murder, the defendant was found - Guilty.

The defence attorney was furious. He waited, and when he saw the foreman of the jury leaving the court building, he rudely broached him, "How the hell did you return a verdict of guilty? I watched the jury, and you were looking at the door to the courtroom. You must have had at least an element of doubt."

The jury's foreman was crystal clear when he responded. "You are correct, sir. Most of the jury was watching the door to the court, but I wasn't. I was looking at your client, and that murderin' sonofabitch wasn't looking at no door. I will bid you a good day, sir."

Well, that brings me to the end of my police memoirs. After almost twenty-eight years in the West Midlands Police, it was time to move on.

In 2016, Tommy was a National Swimming champion (200-metre Freestyle, 13 and under), which allowed me to boast - "I have two children. One swims, the other flies."

Peter wrote on 19 June 2023 - 'Today is my last working day in the Royal Air Force before I officially exit the service twenty-two years after I joined. I've been lucky enough to qualify on Bulldogs, Tutors, Tucanos, Tornado F3s, PC-21s and three variants of the Hawk.
Though I did not set out to spend most of my career instructing, that's what I have done since 2009. I feel privileged to have been involved in the lives of so many talented individuals. I am genuinely sorry to leave that part of my life behind, albeit I will continue

to fly and instruct in warmer climes!' I hope Peter will write his memoirs one day. I would love to read them.

Though I have called this book Further Disclosure, I think of it more as Full Disclosure's little brother.

Well, that is all from me. Hang on, did I ever tell you about the time…

THE END

Hi, I hope you enjoyed I my book.
Can I ask you to consider leaving a review on -
Amazon.co.uk
If you would like to order signed paperback copies of
- Full Disclosure or Further Disclosure.
Message me at wolfiesmith427@gmail.com
Many thanks
Vince Smith

Printed in Great Britain
by Amazon